W9-CCO-164

FREAKIN'
FABULOUS

FREAKIN'
FABU

SIMON SPOTLIGHT ENTERTAINMENT
New York London Toronto Sydney

CLINTON

LOUS

HOW TO **DRESS, SPEAK, BEHAVE, EAT, DRINK, ENTERTAIN, DECORATE,** AND GENERALLY **BE BETTER** THAN EVERYONE ELSE

SIMON SPOTLIGHT ENTERTAINMENT
AN IMPRINT OF SIMON AND SCHUSTER
1230 AVENUE OF THE AMERICAS, NEW YORK, NEW YORK 10020
 • Designed by Jane Archer (www.psbella.com)

Manufactured in the United States of America • First Edition 10 9 8 7 6 5 4 3 2
Library of Congress Cataloging-in-Publication Data: Kelly, Clinton. Freakin' fabulous : how to dress, speak, behave, eat, drink, entertain, decorate, and generally be better than everyone else / Clinton Kelly. — 1st ed.
p. cm.
ISBN-13: 978-1-4169-6149-9 (hardcover)
ISBN-10: 1-4169-6149-6 (hardcover)
1. Etiquette. 2. Manners and customs. 3. Success. I. Title.
BJ1853.K45 2008
646.7—dc22 2008027576

This book is dedicated to all the people who recognized, encouraged, and contributed to my fabulousness over the years. They include—but are by no means limited to:

Mike, Terri, Jodi, Courtney, Annette, Mike, Kona, Maureen, Pawk, Meredith, Jennifer, and, of course, Damon.

It is with sincere thanks to you that I learned my 12 most cherished life lessons:

1. Truly good people sometimes wear really bad denim shorts.
2. Dress up a little to go to the dentist.
3. Every car trip goes faster when you sing.
4. Sometimes the floor of a Parisian hotel bathroom is the best place for stinky cheese and a heart-to-heart.
5. If you want to make someone really happy, have a surprise plate of warm pork chops and sauerkraut waiting on the table for him when he gets home from work.
6. Grow your own peas.
7. When reading a child's tea leaves, tell him you see an important letter being delivered. Then, send him a letter.
8. Even the prettiest ducks can be ferocious.
9. At least once a year, you must lie at the ocean's edge and let the waves break over you.
10. Spying on people might be fun, but it's also wrong.
11. Don't drink and dial.
12. Love beyond.

CONTENTS

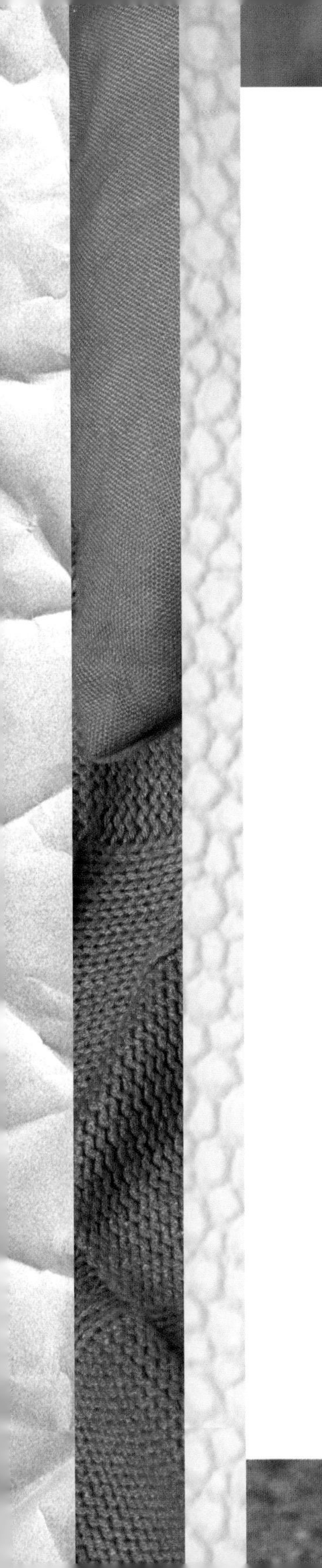

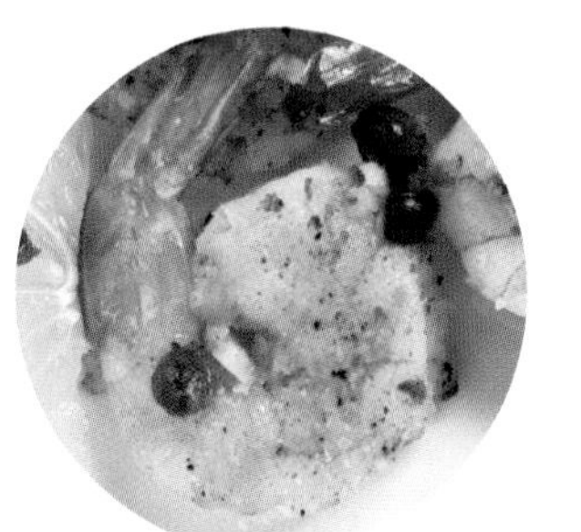

From the Desk of
CLINTON KELLY

My journey toward fabulousness began early; we're talking pre-puberty.

While other kids on the elementary school playground were trading baseball cards and playing kickball, I was silently debating whether to spend my first paycheck on Italian suede driving shoes or on a cashmere coat.

While I waited to be called into the pediatrician's office for my yearly physical, I would glance up from the inevitable copy of *Highlights* magazine and mentally rearrange the paintings of freakishly large-eyed children and suspicious clowns hanging on the walls.

At a friend's ninth birthday party, I inadvertently insulted the host's mother by informing her that her deviled egg yolks were overly mayonnaised and would probably benefit from the inclusion of some finely minced celery, as the other moms traded subtle nods of agreement.

It hasn't been an easy trip. And it's certainly not over. Every once in a while, I'll wake up in a cold sweat because I've realized that a thank-you note I mailed the day before contained a dangling modifier. Or I'll spend too much time wondering why one of my party guests didn't finish the Manhattan I made her. (Did I use too much sweet vermouth? Did she not like my choice of bourbon? Is she in AA again?) If I let myself, I can spend the whole day fantasizing about the head-to-toe makeovers I would give passersby, with or without their consent. I doubt this is normal. Oh well.

I've written this book for two reasons. And one of them isn't even "for the money."

The first is to help the huddled masses yearning to be fabulous. Someone's got to teach them life's most important lessons about aesthetics and behavior and gastronomy. It might as well be me. I mean . . . it might as well be I.

The second is to get all this crap out of my head. I figure if I write all this information down and style pretty pictures to accompany it, I can get on with my life. It's like emptying the hard drive on a computer to make room for new information. Who knows, perhaps I'll free up space to achieve new levels of fabulousness. Or maybe I'll get a degree in physics and invent something important, like X-ray specs that actually work. Or maybe I'll finally convince JoBeth Williams, the glamorous star of *Poltergeist*, that I'm not a freak and she should answer my letters, especially the ones inquiring which conditioner she uses to keep her hair looking so soft and luxurious.

Anyway, I hope you'll get something out of this. If only one more person on this planet learns how to make a delightful hollandaise from scratch, I'll consider myself a success. Actually, that's a lie. I will only feel successful when I sell five million copies of this book and Congress passes a law deeming the possession of a Hummel collection a crime punishable by a vigorous shaking about the shoulders and a sound talking-to.

Godspeed,

Clinton

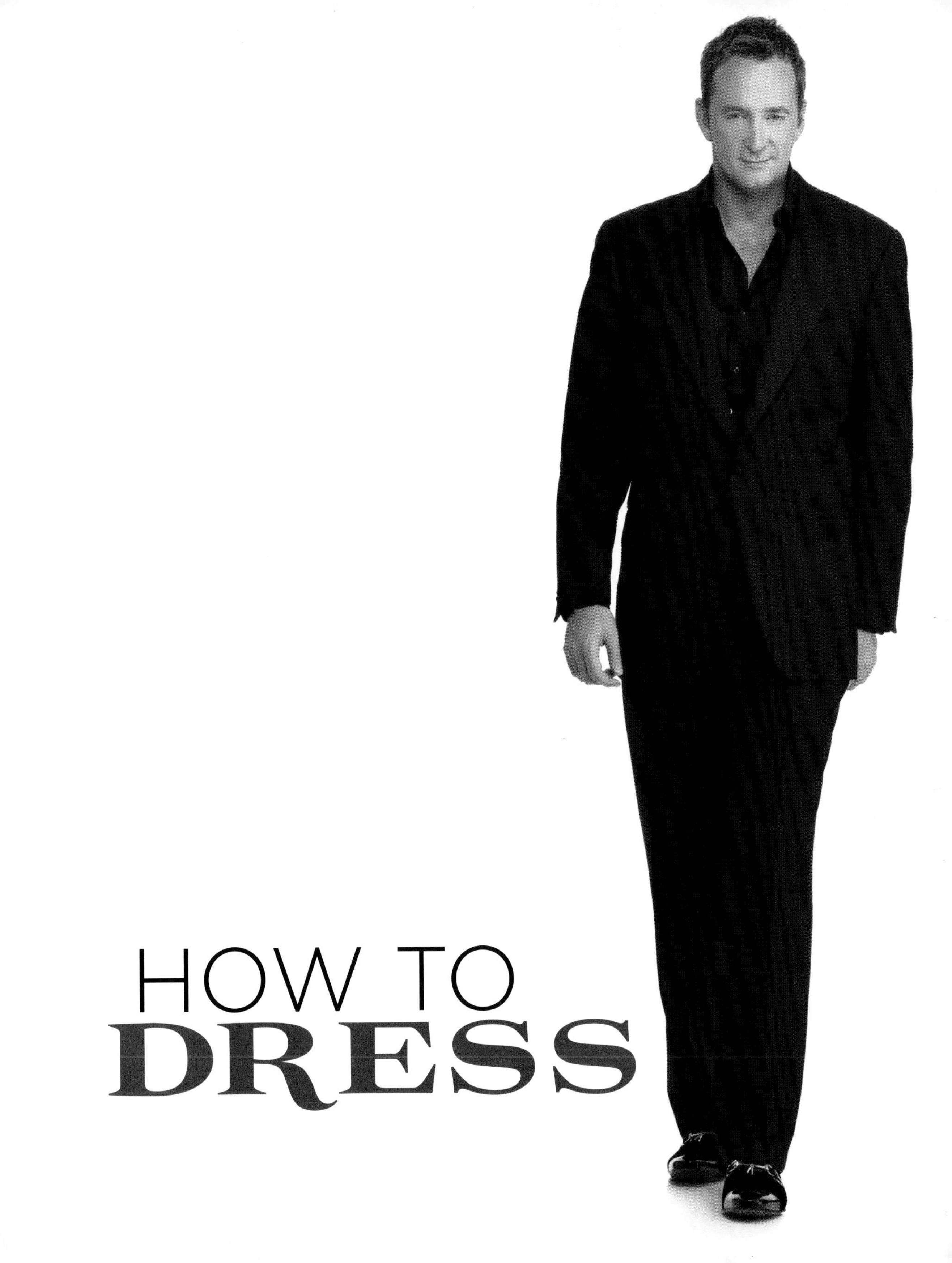
HOW TO
DRESS

As you can tell by the ridiculously long subtitle of this book, fabulousness requires mastery—or at least *perceived* mastery—of topics ranging from style to manners to gastronomy to décor.

I'll begin by teaching you some of the most important components of style because, quite frankly, if you look like hell, nobody will ever find you fabulous. People might say, "Oh, that Mary sure throws an amazing party. Did you know she speaks six languages? And isn't it swell how she single-handedly rescued that busload of blind children from the Mississippi River?" But they will never use the word "fabulous" to describe you if you did it all while wearing tapered acid-washed jeans.

I've said it hundreds of times before and I will say it hundreds more, I'm sure: **"What you wear tells the world how you expect to be treated."** And take it from me, being treated as though you're fabulous is *way* better than being treated like a schmuck.

So, I want you to forget everything your mama taught you about how to dress yourself. I am your new mama. **But you can call me Big Daddy . . .** I like that.

Let's start with the basics. There are three concepts without a clear understanding of which you cannot achieve style. (Now might be a good time to differentiate between fashion and style. "Fashion" is what designers create and sell. You know, clothes, shoes, bags, and other accessories. "Style" is your usage and interpretation of what is available to you. Does that make sense? Good, it should. Or I'd be really concerned about your capacity for absorbing more complex ideas like where babies come from.)

The three main components of style are:

---

1. FIT
2. PROPORTION
3. APPROPRIATENESS

Let's tackle them one by one.

FIT

If you don't have fit, you don't have style. End of story.

Clothes that are tight can make you appear bigger. When a garment clings to some area of your body, it's like that body part is screaming, "Look at me! Look at me! Do you see how I refuse to be constrained?!" Now, that's not always a bad thing. You might actually want to don a tight sweater to draw attention to your boobs. But I, for one, don't want everyone staring at the 10 squishy pounds that have settled around my navel. That's why I avoid spandex muscle tees.

Clothes that are too loose can also make you appear bigger. Very often, women will tell me that they're trying to camouflage what they consider a large butt by wearing drapey tops that completely cover it. But if your clothes look baggy and shapeless, people will assume that what's under them is just as baggy and shapeless. Don't believe me? Let's take a look at the following photographs.

Here's Agnes wearing a **size 4** when she's actually about a **size 8.**

What's your first impression of Agnes? I'll tell you mine, just off the top of my head, because that's what I do: This chick thinks she's smaller than she actually is, leading me to believe that she has a skewed sense of reality in general. I'm guessing she thinks that *Survivor* is real. I also feel a little sorry for her. Perhaps it's because she's stuck in the past. Maybe she bought this outfit last year but has since had a bad breakup and found solace in a few too many tubes of raw cookie dough.

Now, here's Agnes, still a size 8, wearing a size 16.

My first impressions: What a dumpy, shlumpy mess. I'm guessing that her kids are the ones on the playground with the snot-encrusted noses and matted hair. She also hates her body ever since her husband left her and started a new family in Akron. Someone give this woman a towel so she can throw it in.

Here's Agnes wearing clothes that fit!

My new first impressions of Agnes: Wow, this woman is intelligent, charming, and put-together. She's obviously a devoted wife, a nurturing mother, and a successful businesswoman. Plus, she runs a small nonprofit that saves hundreds of baby seals and 12 acres of rainforest a week! How does she do it all?

Isn't this game fun?

Now meet Fred. He has an average build, but here he's wearing clothes that are too tight.

My first impressions of Fred: Instead of drinking beer and eating pork rinds all day, he should get his ass to the gym. And what's up with those pants? They're so tight I can practically see his pulse. Freak show.

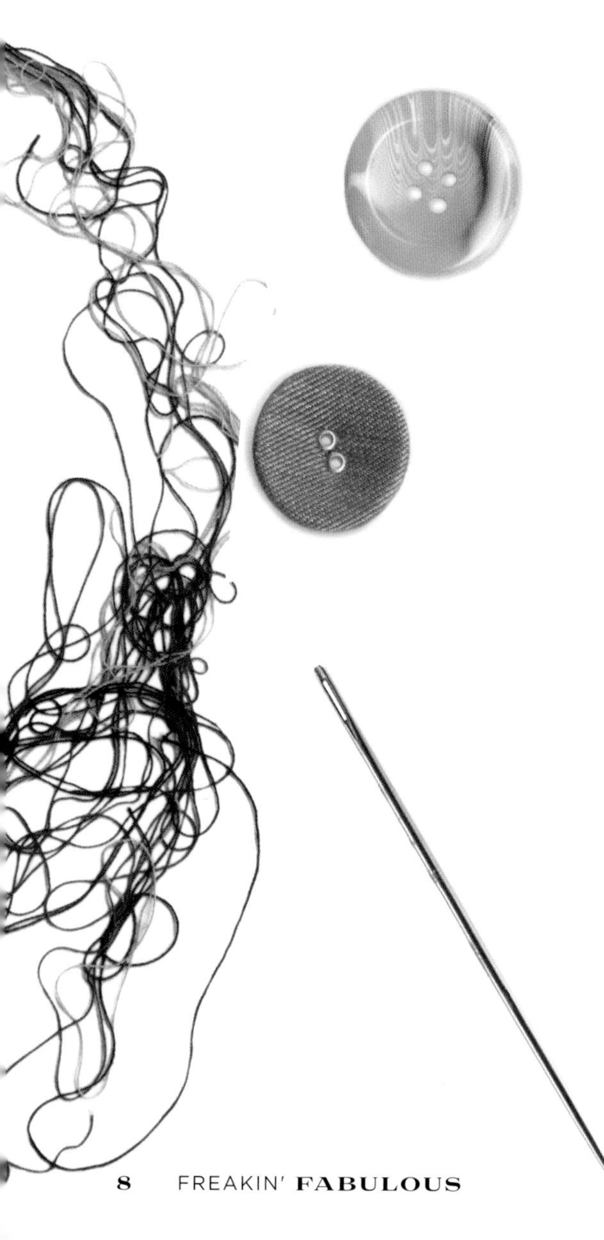

Here's Fred wearing **oversized clothes.**

What this look says about Fred: Fred is your average American male who thinks he is an XL because if he admits to himself that he has a medium-size frame, he will have to come to terms with the size of his "average" penis.

Here's Fred in clothes that fit!

What this look says about Fred: Ladies, form an orderly queue! He can't decide which of you to marry when you're all pushing and shoving like that. Boy, Fred sure has it all: snazzy clothes, a job that fulfills him financially and spiritually, and a dynamite sense of humor. He may have an average-size penis—but he sure knows how to use it!

HOW TO FIND CLOTHES THAT FIT

The sooner you realize we're living in a capitalist society, the sooner you will cease living a life filled with disappointment and despair, at least at the mall. See, designers and manufacturers want to make money, and to make money you have to sell clothes, and to sell lots of clothes you need to manufacture garments that fit as many body types as possible.

In case you haven't noticed, people come in countless combinations of sizes, shapes, and proportions. Some people have big asses, some people have legs that meet their backs with nary a bump along the way. Some women have gigantic ta-tas, and some are built like Sheetrock. Some people are tall (like me—6-foot-4), and some people are so small you could carry them around in a Birkin bag. Cute!

Here's a very official-looking graph that will demonstrate my point. (Sorry it's on a bar nap. It was all I had available.) If we were to chart every American woman's height and weight on an x and y axis, we would get something like this:

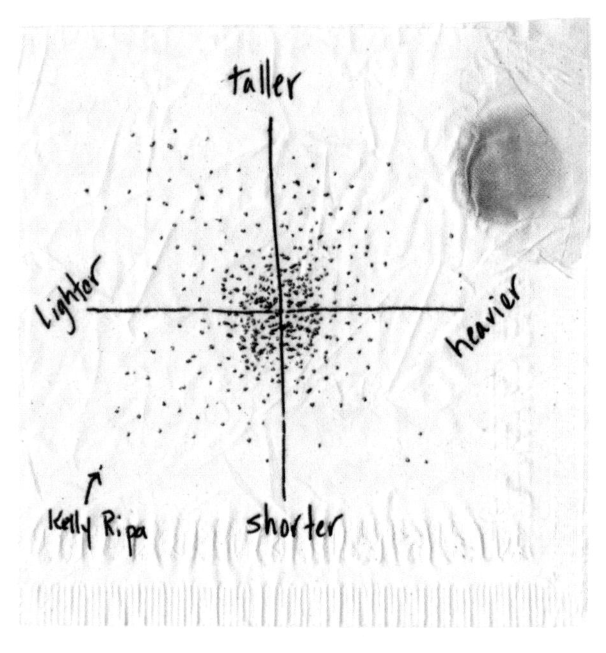

QUESTION: How can one structured jacket fit all those dots?

ANSWER: It can't. Duh.

THEREFORE, IT IS **UNREASONABLE** FOR YOU TO EXPECT GARMENTS TO FIT YOU PERFECTLY OFF THE RACK. AND IF YOU THINK I AM YELLING AT YOU IN PRINT, THAT'S BECAUSE **I AM**. I CANNOT STRESS ENOUGH THE IMPORTANCE OF BUYING THE CORRECT SIZE AND HAVING A GOOD TAILOR. THESE TWO THINGS MAKE THE DIFFERENCE BETWEEN **MEDIOCRITY** AND **FABULOSITY**.

Most of the time, clothes will "almost" fit. And you cannot have style when clothes "almost" fit. It's like being an "almost" lawyer when everyone knows you failed the bar three times and you should just go back to working for your dad.

Sometimes things will fit right off the rack, but most of the time they won't. When something "almost" fits, you have two options:

---

1. **Try on more stuff** until you find something that "actually" fits.

2. **Take it to a tailor** and make it "actually" fit.

Here are some common **"almost"** fits and how to fix them if at all possible.

BAGGY CROTCH *Possibly Fixable*

Ladies and gentlemen, the crotch of your pants should sit pretty darn close to your anatomical crotch, or as the kids these days call it, your "junk." It should not droop halfway down to your knee, even if your anatomical junk does. A baggy crotch is usually a symptom of a loose-fitting waist, because if the pants were sitting higher on the waist, the crotch would also be higher. Right? Right. So have a tailor hike the waist of the pants up a bit and take it in, and the pants and crotch will hang where they should.

X-MARKS-THE-SPOT CROTCH *Not Fixable*

Sorry, babe. That crisscross on your crotch is telling the world that your pants are too tight in the thigh, butt, or both. You'll have to go up a size until you find pants that hang smoothly over the crotch and thigh. I'll tell you now: They'll be too big in the waist, so you'll have to have them taken in. Annoying? Yes. But so are most children.

ANYTHING YOU CAN'T BUTTON

Not Fixable

You would think this little tip is obvious, but some people are knuckleheads. I know this because I've made a nice living by publicly making fun of them. Let me explain this for the 5,934th time: **ANYTHING YOU CAN'T BUTTON, BUCKLE, OR FASTEN DOES NOT FIT YOU AND THEREFORE YOU SHOULD NOT WEAR IT.** Go up a size before I throw this beer can at your head.

GAP IN THE BACK

Fixable

This is probably the most common frustration expressed by my female clients. When you have a small waist-to-hip ratio, meaning your waist measurement is significantly smaller than that of your hip and/or butt, you'll have what my friend Shannon refers to as "room for a party" in the back. The good news is, this is an easy alteration. Just ask your tailor to nip the waist, then go wipe up the dance floor with that hot boo-tay.

DROOPY SHOULDERS

Fixable

I can't stand a droopy shoulder. I think it makes people look suicidal. In fact, sometimes I want to give someone wearing a droopy shoulder a bottle of pills and say, "Go for it!" But I like my pills too much to part with them. The shoulder seam of a garment should sit on the outside edge of your shoulder. If it extends down your arm, try one size smaller. Or if it's a jacket that you purchased in a larger size because you needed it to close (see "Anything You Can't Button"), ask your tailor to reset the shoulder.

Note: Every once in a while, a dropped shoulder will become trendy. But as with any trend, make sure it works with your body type and lifestyle.

PEEKABOO BUTTONS

Possibly Fixable

Nothing says "I've put on a few pounds" like a glimpse of flesh between the buttons of your shirt. If those spaces are really gaping, you probably need to go up a size. But if the shirt fits and there's just a little window into your cleavage, you can add a snap or a little Velcro tab to keep the shirt together.

VISIBLE PANTY LINE *Usually Fixable*

VPL gets a lot of press these days. It's pretty much the media whore of fashion mishaps. Sometimes VPL occurs because of a problem with fit and sometimes it happens because you're wearing big ole nasty panties. First, try switching undergarments. Spanx or other shapers should smooth things out, or if those make you feel like a stuffed sausage, your other option is America's favorite butt floss, the thong. If both those options are objectionable, you need to go up a size in your pants or go commando. Sorry, but it's the truth.

BAGGY JACKET *Usually Fixable*

Sometimes you'll find a totally cute jacket that closes comfortably and rests nicely on the shoulder but isn't so flattering through the midsection. Fret not. Most jackets have seams that run under the armhole to the hem, along which your tailor can narrow the garment. But do yourself a favor and avoid jackets with low armholes because they just make you look dumpy.

BAGGY SHIRT *Fixable*

The worst thing a man—or a woman for that matter—with a narrow frame can do is wear a loose-fitting button-front shirt. Instead of looking thin, you'll look scrawny. (I'd illustrate this point with a photo of myself from junior high school, but I burned them all years ago.) Buy slim-fit shirts when you can, or ask your tailor to add darts up the back. Women with larger bazooms might also need darts created under the bust line.

SLEEVES TOO LONG *Totally Fixable*

A sleeve that is too long makes you look messy and your hand look weirdly stubby. A man's jacket sleeve should cover his wrist and not extend onto his hand. The shirt sleeve should extend a half inch past the jacket sleeve. A woman's jacket can be a little longer, or a little shorter, or a lot shorter. (See "Length Matters.")

LENGTH MATTERS

When it comes to the rules about sleeve and pant lengths, women have a few more options than men. Try as designers might, they just can't get the American male to embrace the bracelet-length sleeve worn with pedal pushers.

WOMEN:

The following are acceptable lengths for jacket and shirt sleeves:

- *Bracelet length*
- *Three-quarter length*
- *Standard length*
- *And pretty much anything in between*

The following are acceptable lengths for pants:

- *Pedal pusher*
- *Clam digger*
- *Cropped*
- *Regular old pants*
- *And pretty much anything in between*

Some notes on lengths:

- *Cropped pants aren't always so flattering on petites because they can make your legs look a little stumpy. I've found through extensive research that a cropped pant is most flattering when it hits just below the widest part of the calf.*
- *Wide- or straight-leg jeans look best when they're just skimming the floor but not dragging. Skinny jeans look best when they hit at the ankle.*

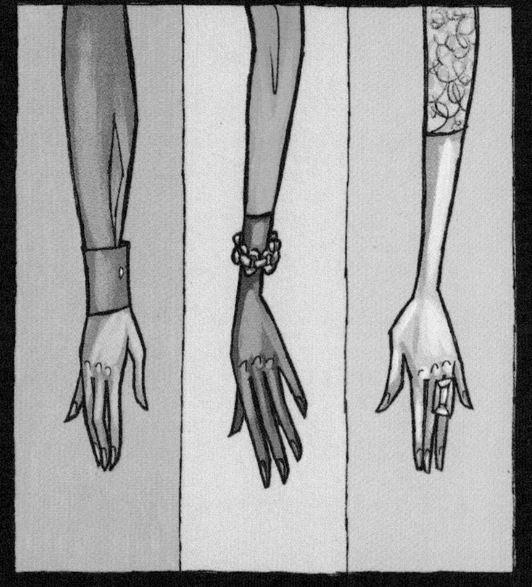

- *Contrary to popular belief, jeans can indeed be hemmed! To avoid the Mom-shortened-these-for-me look, ask your tailor to attach the original hem, if possible, or use gold-colored thread and scuff up the new hem with a little sandpaper.*

MEN:

- *Your jacket sleeve should cover your wrist and only your wrist. Do not let it cover your hand.*
- *Your shirt sleeve should extend exactly one half inch beyond your jacket sleeve. No more, no less.*
- *Your pants should be long enough to cover your socks while walking and form a single break atop your shoes.*

PROPORTION

Now that we've discussed the importance of fit, let's move on to proportion.

Fashion types will occasionally say things like, "Did you see so-and-so's most recent collection? The proportions were all off. He's a hack." Or, "It was genius, pure genius, I tell you, the way she played with proportion this season. By the way, don't you love my shoes? I stole them from the fashion closet at work and blamed it on an intern." When I'm confronted with this kind of gibberish, I just let my eyes glaze over and pretend I'm still a little dizzy from my last purge.

That said, however, there are two important aspects of proportion you need to understand before you can claim to have any sense of style whatsoever:

---

1. The size of **the things you wear** (patterns, bags, accessories) in **relation to the size of your body.**
2. The size of **your body parts** in **relation to each other**.

Simply put, if you have a **smaller frame**, you'll want to **wear things that are smaller**. If you have a **larger frame**, you'll want to **wear things that are larger.**

For Example:

Marie is 5-foot-1 and weighs 100 pounds soaking wet. When she dresses herself in a big abstract print, with huge jewelry and an oversized bag, she looks a little "off," you know, like she spends a lot of time talking to her two cats, Mister Boots and Peeper, and sometimes they talk back.

Now, Marie's outfit isn't walking into the room before she is. When you have a small frame, you should keep your prints, bags, and accessories small. That's just a general rule of thumb. However, as you can see, I've kept Marie in a large print, but the jewelry and bag are smaller. If big bags become the new "must have," she can carry one; she'll just want to keep the jewelry and prints on the smaller side.

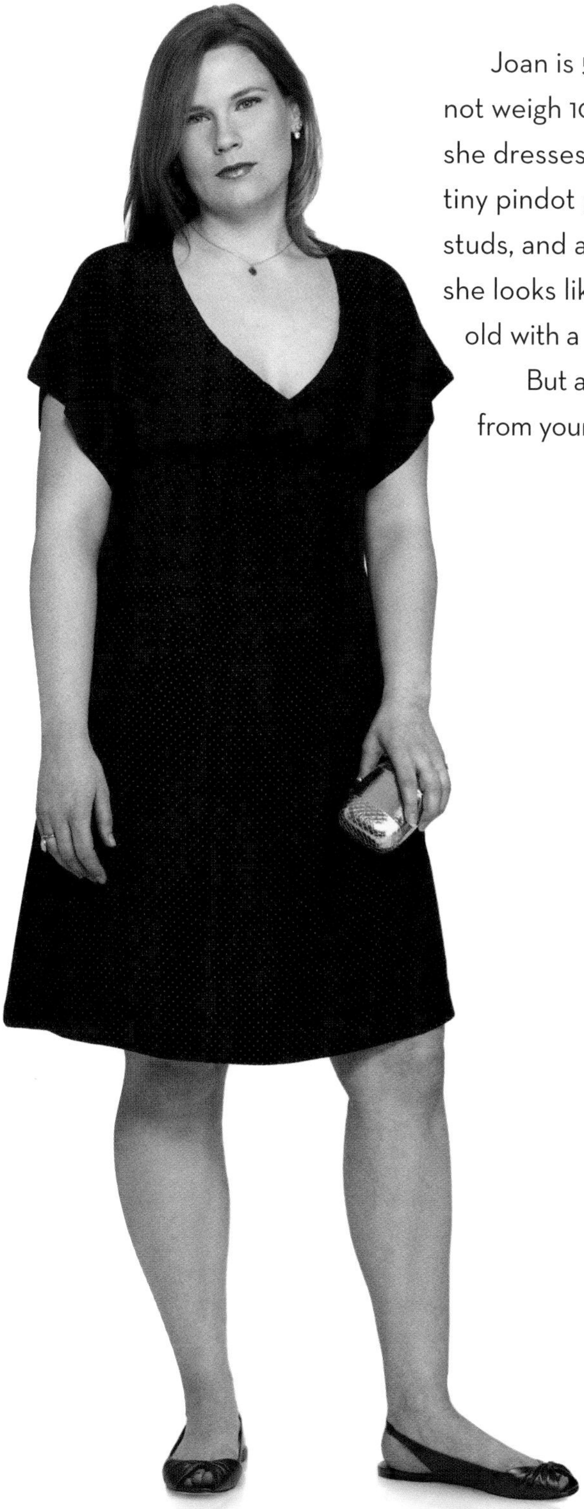

Joan is 5-foot-10 and does not weigh 100 pounds. When she dresses herself in a teeny-tiny pindot print, little diamond studs, and a miniscule clutch, she looks like an Amish 13-year-old with a glandular condition.

But after a little tweaking from yours truly . . .

This bolder tropical print is more in keeping with Joan's stature. I sent the smaller dots packing because they made her appear bigger. (It takes more dots to cover a larger frame.) Her formerly dinky jewelry has been replaced with more substantial pieces. Little studs and thin rings can look cheap on a larger frame and only makes you look bigger in proportion.

With accessories and prints that are consistent with the size of their frames, the women look incredible. You'd never know that one of them has anger-management issues and the other clips her toenails in bed!

Now, what about average-size women? Quite frankly, if you're 5-foot-5 and a size 8, the proportion issues I've just described won't concern you as much. With that said, you should still keep proportion in mind. If you want to wear a small print, that's fine, but you might want to carry a larger bag to balance it out. If you love oversized jewelry, don't pull focus from it by wearing an oversized print.

There's another important aspect of proportion that involves the size of your body parts in relation to one another. The idealized female form has been expressed as an hourglass for centuries: bust and hip measurements that are roughly equal to each other with a narrow waist. Think Botticelli's *Birth of Venus,* Marilyn Monroe, or Britney Spears in "Hit Me Baby One More Time."

For men, the silhouette of a strong shoulder with a narrow waist and streamlined legs has been equally idealized. Think Michelangelo's *David,* Marlon Brando in *A Streetcar Named Desire,* and any number of Abercrombie & Fitch models who will eventually turn 33 and realize that their metabolisms aren't what they used to be and that they'll actually have to learn how to DO something other than stand around with their shirts off and their inguinal ligaments rippling, bulging, and tempting you like that bag of Double Stuf Oreos in the back of the kitchen cupboard. Where was I?

Oh, yes . . . so, following the second principle of proportion, the idea is to wear clothing that tricks the eye into seeing you as perfectly proportioned even if you're not.

If you're large-busted but narrow from the waist down...

This body type is typically referred to as top-heavy, and most women I know don't want to be anything "heavy." Sure, being boobalicious can be fun, but you don't want to give people the impression that you could face-plant at any given moment. The solution is to add more volume or attention to your lower half so that it looks proportionate to your top half.

- **AN A-LINE SKIRT**
- **A PLEATED SKIRT**
- **WIDE-LEG TROUSERS**
- **LIGHTER-COLORED BOTTOMS**

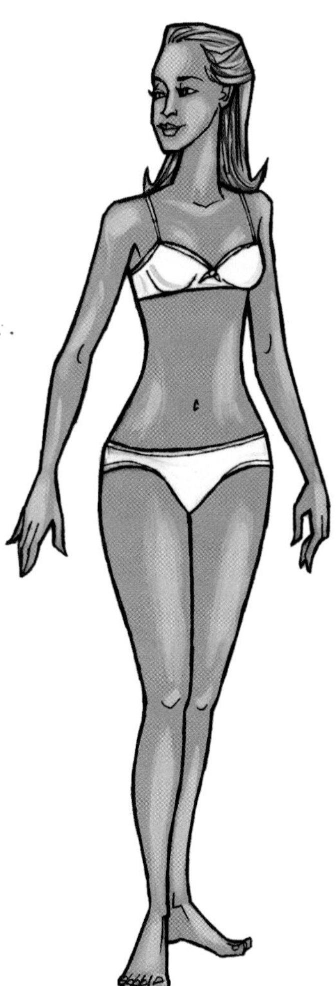

If you're flat-chested but curvaceous from the waist down...

This body type is commonly referred to as pear-shaped, but I don't think it does anyone any good to compare herself to fruits or vegetables—unless we're discussing Paris Hilton's mental acuity. Then, feel free to compare her IQ to that of a summer squash. Anyway, trust me: The best way to take emphasis away from your lower half is by adding emphasis to your top half.

- **SCOOP NECKS**
- **NECKLINE EMBELLISHMENT**
- **HORIZONTAL STRIPES**
- **LIGHTER-COLORED TOPS**

If you've got a tummy . . .

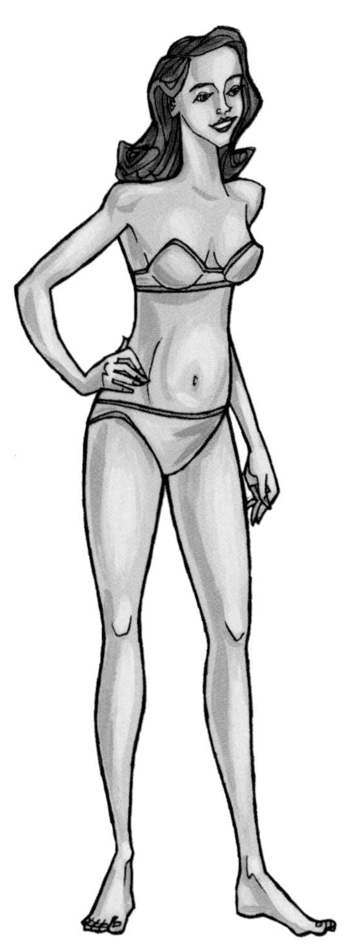

The question I am asked most frequently—by far—is, "How do I camouflage a tummy?" And, look, I get it: If you're a woman and you're carrying weight in your midsection, you probably don't feel as though you're anywhere near that idealized hourglass body type. So the first thing I'm going to tell you is not to freak out. You are certainly not alone. About half of the women I have dressed carry some weight in the tummy. For some women, it's the first place they gain a few pounds. Others see changes after giving birth or after menopause. It's not the end of the world, not even close. And it's certainly not a good reason to give up on style.

The best way to camouflage a tummy is with a jacket. Hands down. Don't even try to argue with me because I will win. In fact, I will mop the floor with you.

The right jacket will strengthen a shoulder, which balances out a midsection. The right jacket will also have some seaming and darting, which will create the illusion of an hourglass waistline, even if you don't have one.

Blazers can also create the illusion of verticality on the body because of the V that's created by the lapels. This extra visual "height" helps balance out a little width.

Now, some of you are undoubtedly saying to yourselves, "Sometimes it's too hot for a jacket."

True. If so, the next-best way to camouflage a tummy is with a shirt or blouse that floats away from the body, like an empire-seamed top. Now, I hear some of you saying, "But I feel like I'm pregnant in an empire-seamed top."

OK, well, that's understandable because maternity tops often have empire seams. So, I'd encourage you to look for empire-seamed tops that are not heavily ruched or pleated under the bust. Think of it as an A-line skirt from the seam down.

And if all else fails, wear a tunic, the coverer of all sins.

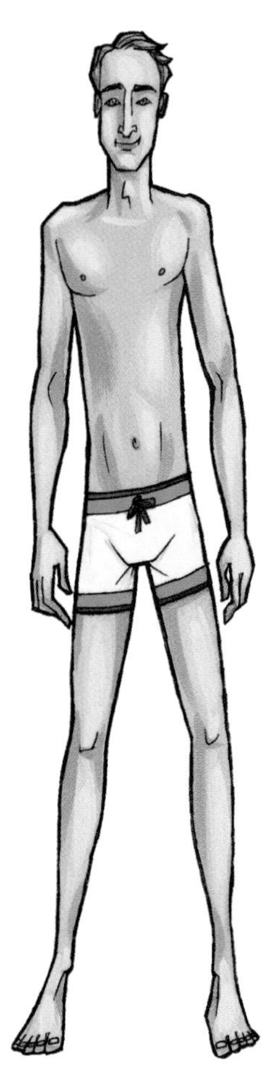

If you've got narrow shoulders...

That classic V shape is hard to achieve if you're built like a lowercase 1. I should know because that's the shape I had for about 30 years. You might want to avoid monochromatic looks because they'll emphasize your narrowness. Add some emphasis to your top half with:

- **HORIZONTAL STRIPES**
- **JACKETS**
- **PATTERN**
- **RAGLAN SLEEVES**

If you've got a gut...

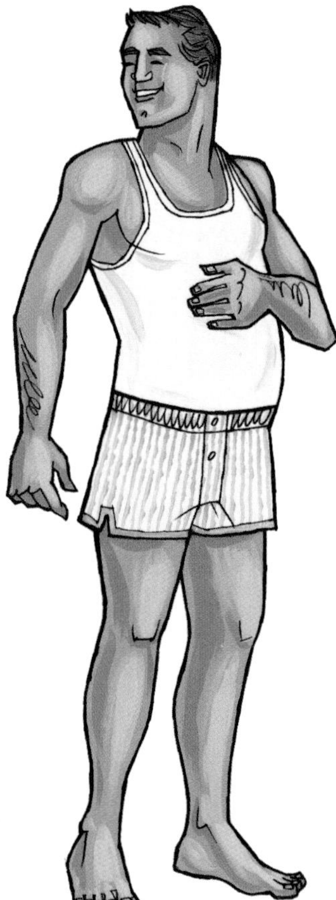

I've told the ladies this already, but it's worth repeating: The best way to camouflage a tummy is with a jacket. A good jacket will take the emphasis away from the midsection and bring it to the shoulder.

- **JACKETS**
- **MONOCHROMATIC LOOKS**
- **UNTUCKED SHIRTS WHEN APPROPRIATE**

Tucking a shirt will usually draw attention to the gut. This can be offset by topping your outfit with a jacket. But for casualwear, you can leave your shirt untucked. Just make sure the shirt isn't too long. A shirt that covers the crotch will visually shorten the leg. If your legs look shorter, you look shorter. If you look shorter, you look wider.

If you carry your weight in your lower half...

Sometimes a man carries his weight in his lower half, which can be a little feminizing even if you're a total macho stud. The best thing to do is shift the emphasis to the top half of your body and lengthen the lower.

- **DARK BOTTOMS**
- **LIGHT TOPS**
- **JACKETS, YET AGAIN**
- **PINSTRIPE PANTS**

ASSORTED OTHER BODY TYPE CONCERNS

On the preceding pages, I addressed the concept of proportion, specifically how to create the illusion of an hourglass shape for women and a V shape for men. Now, let's tackle some other issues.

If you're a woman with no curves...

You can take comfort in the fact that most runway models don't have curves either. Women with this body type often have the easiest time wearing high-end designer clothes. The best advice I can offer you is to use volume to create the illusion of curves but be very careful not to be overwhelmed by it. For example, you could wear a full skirt, but pair it with a top that fits close to the body. Or, wear a ruffled top, but pair it with a skinny jean. Women with thin frames can look scrawny if their clothes are oversized or just hang on the body.

If you're a woman with lots of curves and an hourglass shape . . .

I highly recommend doing everything in your power to emphasize your waistline. Look for wrap dresses, faux-wrap tops, anything with a belt or a seam to bring attention to your narrowest part. You've got the ideal shape, so show it off.

If you're a woman with lots of curves and a tummy . . .

I'll be honest with you: Your body type is one of the most challenging to dress. I don't say that to make you feel bad about yourself; it's just that, for whatever reason, most designers aren't creating clothes with you in mind. I'd like to see that change. In the meantime, I want you to look for clothes with STRUCTURE. The average T-shirt has two seams, one under each arm. That is not enough. Look for blouses that have darts under the bust and seams that create a waist. Instead of covering yourself in an oversized button-front shirt, wear a lightweight jacket. And when it comes to dresses, go for deep V-necks, defined waistlines, and skirts that float away from the body.

If you've got thick thighs...

The best way to camouflage them is with an A-line skirt. Second best: wide-leg trousers.

If you've got cankles and you want to wear a dress...

This one's a toughie. First of all, never, ever wear an ankle-strap shoe. While a high heel will narrow the ankle's appearance a bit, a super-sexy shoe will draw the eye down to your cankles. So, look for a dress that brings attention upward and a shoe that blends. If you have cocoa skin, wear a brown pointy-toe. If you're beige, try a nude patent shoe. If you are still not comfortable with the way you look in a dress, a pair of tuxedo pants and a sparkly top can be very chic for evening.

If you've got thick calves...

Look for a dress with a skirt that floats away from the body and hits just below the knee. Avoid embellished hems. Instead, wear solid colors on the bottom and use embellished necklines to draw attention upward. As for cropped pants, have them hemmed to about an inch or so below the widest part of the calf.

If you've got Bingo Wings (a.k.a. plump arms)...

When you carry your weight in your upper arms, you may find the sleeves of many garments to be too narrow. Generally, I tell clients with this issue to look for lightweight knits, preferably a spandex blend, which will stretch slightly to accommodate larger arms. If it's too warm to wear a knit, look for lightweight tunics that have kimono-style sleeves; they'll provide nonbinding coverage. Many short-sleeve shirts can also be altered to fit a larger arm. I have often asked tailors to cut a banded sleeve and add either a button-and-loop closure on the outside of the sleeve or some hidden elastic on the underside.

If you've got narrow Shoulders and a large bust...

It's pretty rare that I'll recommend a shoulder pad, but in this instance they can be incredibly helpful. A larger chest looks more at home on a larger shoulder, or at least a straight shoulder. If your shoulders have a natural slope, you can appear as though the weight of your bust is pulling you down. Ask your tailor to reinforce the shoulders of your jacket with quarter-inch pads—not with Linda Evans–style pads—and your body will look more balanced.

Where the Boobs Are

When I'm speaking to a large audience about style, I will occasionally get bored of listening to myself yammer on about structured jackets and medium-rise, dark-wash, straight-leg jeans. So, I will abruptly change the subject by declaring, "Do you know what time it is? It's time to talk about your boobies!" Nervous giggles inevitably erupt.

I'll say, "The most significant thing a woman can do to change her silhouette is to be professionally fitted for a bra. It's true! Nine times out of ten, a woman's narrowest part is under the bust—if her boobs are sitting in the ideal spot. Would you like to know where the ideal spot is?"

Eyes widen and heads nod. Some women will even plead, "Please, Clinton, tell us!"

And I continue, "For the ideal silhouette, your breasts should hit halfway between your shoulder and your elbow."

This next part amuses the crap out of me. Inevitably, I will see the tops of many heads as women gaze down at their chests, and I make a mental note about the collective IQ of the group because I like to judge people. It makes me feel smarter.

"No, no, no," I say. "You can't see where your own boobs hit by looking down at them! You have to go home, strip down to your bra, and look in the mirror! Or better yet, you can invite a friend over and have her draw a line on your arm with a Sharpie and write, 'YOUR BOOBS HIT HERE.' If your line is in the crease of your elbow, you need to hoist those babies up. If your line is on your shoulder, you need a new plastic surgeon."

Then we all just tip our heads back and laugh and laugh. . . . But seriously, when shopping for a bra, you need to be fitted by someone who has been professionally trained, not a 16-year-old who's got a part-time job at the mall. When fitting themselves, most women make the mistake of buying a bra that's too small in the cup and too big in the band. With a good bra, most of the work is done by the band, not the straps. That band should be snug but comfortable, and it shouldn't pinch. If you can fit one finger between the band and your body, you're probably on the right track. If the straps are digging into your shoulders, that's a sign that the band isn't doing enough of the work and you might have to go down one band size.

APPROPRIATENESS

Knowing what to wear when is the third component of true style in my book, the book that you're reading now.
Let me explain.

You might have a beautiful white dress that fits you perfectly, and all of your accessories may be perfectly proportioned. But if you wear that white dress to your sister's wedding, you are a complete and total beee-otch. (Unless your sister is marrying the boyfriend she stole from you while you were on a business trip to Fargo. Then, by all means, you should wear a short, hot white dress while making a toast that includes the words *skank* and *flaccid*.)

Or here's another example: You might have a beautiful red minidress that fits you perfectly, and all of your accessories may be perfectly proportioned. But if you wear that red minidress to your 86-year-old lover's funeral, you are a hosebag.

In this section, we will cover the two main types of appropriateness:

- **AGE APPROPRIATENESS**
- **SITUATIONAL APPROPRIATENESS**

I've already answered the question I'm asked most frequently (How do you camouflage a tummy?), so now I'll answer the question I am asked second-most frequently, "How do I participate in trends after a certain age?" I find this question to be a lot less tedious, but I'm sure in a few years it will catch up.

If you are concerned that you may be too old to participate in trends, you probably *are* too old to participate in SOME trends, because if you feel uncomfortable in an outfit, you will exude self-consciousness—the ultimate style crusher. However, you should never, ever feel too old to participate in popular fashion culture on some level.

TIME FOR A GAME!

I'm going to list 10 hypothetical trends that may be in style during any given season. It's your job to identify which ones are **appropriate** for a woman over "a certain age."*

(Answers on opposite page.)

1. CROCODILE BAGS

2. TRUMPET SKIRTS

3. SEQUINS

4. RED SHOES

5. TUBE TOPS

6. SHORT SHORTS

7. HERRINGBONE

8. COCKTAIL RINGS

9. BABYDOLL DRESSES

10. LUCITE STILETTOS

* If you think for a second that I'm going to give you a number to define "a certain age," you're crazy. For some women it will be 35; for others, 75. You'll have to make up your own mind on this one, babe.

Answer: 1, 2, 3, 4, 7, 8. Answer if you're Cher, Dolly Parton, or Tina Turner: 1–10.

The rules really aren't that difficult to comprehend. After "a certain age," don't show too much of your breasts or your navel or your inner thighs. (That explains numbers 5, 6, and 9.) Doing so makes you look like you're competing with 22-year-olds. And trust me, you do not want to go there—because 22-year-olds, with their perky breasts, supple skin, and flat abs ALWAYS WIN. It's best to take the high road and continually remind yourself that "life experience" is just as attractive as physical perfection. (Of course, that's a lie, but you would not *believe* the crap you can get your brain to swallow with enough repetition.)

The other rule is: Ask yourself, "Would a partially toothless hooker named Whistles enjoy this trend?" If so, avoid it like the clap. (See number 10.) Other examples of whore-tastic trends, should they ever become stylish: microminis, any garment made of rubber, and T-shirts that say things like, "Moustache rides gladly accepted." Once again, it's best to take the high road and let the world think you're classy, even if you are easier than the *Star* magazine crossword puzzle.

Now, let's discuss situational appropriateness.

Here's my comprehensive guide to What to Wear When. . . . And by "comprehensive" I mean "abbreviated."

AT WORK, IN CORPORATE ENVIRONMENTS

When you work for The Man, you have to play The Game, if you'd prefer not to spend the rest of your life sitting in that cubicle next to the fax machine. I played The Game through most of the 1990s and I think it's fun! Mostly because I have no soul. To be a real player in The Game, you must spend countless hours at the office, kiss lots of ass, and occasionally stab a good friend in the back. You must also "look the part." In other words, try to look like the kind of guy your boss wants to take to the country club. Or the type of woman who eats male chauvinist pigs for breakfast.

AT WORK, IN CREATIVE ENVIRONMENTS

People who work in advertising, publishing, entertainment, and the like have more wardrobial leeway than most. (Do you like how I just made up the word "wardrobial"? I'm really clever like that. Once, when playing Scrabble, I invented the word "quexity" and scored 97 points. My six-year-old nephew never knew what hit him!) However, a job in a creative work environment does not give you permission to look like a slob.

AT WORK, IN TECH ENVIRONMENTS

Like anyone even cares what you people wear. Just get the Diet Coke out of my keyboard and go home to your video games.

AT THE THEATER

Right at this very moment, hundreds of actors in New York City are busting their asses to remember dialogue and dance steps and blocking, just so you can tell your friends back home you saw a show on Broadway. And how do you repay them? (Besides forking over 150 bucks for a ticket to a show that was once an animated movie.) By showing up in a Mickey Mouse T-shirt, faded jeans, and a pair of white sneakers you stole from Richard Simmons? I don't think so.

DAY WEDDING

Daytime weddings are nice. I mean, they're a nice excuse to get plastered in the daytime. When getting dressed for midday nuptials, it's important to remember the overall feeling the bride and groom were probably trying to create when they decided to tie the knot in broad daylight: light, airy, gay (but not in the queer way). When you show up looking like Morticia Addams, you're basically telling the happy couple, "Congratulations, you've started down a path of shared misery and unmet expectations," which may be true, but it's best if they discover that for themselves, God bless 'em.

EVENING WEDDING

Evening weddings are nice. I mean, they're a nice excuse to get plastered in the evening. When dressing for an evening reception, it's important to remember the overall feeling the bride and groom were probably trying to create when they booked the church basement for Saturday from 8 p.m. to midnight: glamorous, sophisticated, chic. When you show up looking like Mary Sunshine in a yellow floral halter dress, you're basically telling the happy couple, "Lithium tastes yummy!"

BLACK-TIE EVENTS

Black tie means men are expected to wear black tuxedos and black ties. Could you get away with wearing a black suit with a black tie? Probably, but you shouldn't. You're definitely better off wearing a well-fitting black suit than an ill-fitting rental with a faint aroma of aged gouda. Not too long ago, black tie meant long dresses for women, and in some circles it still does. Most of the time, however, a woman can wear whatever length dress she chooses. But I recommend that if you're attending a fancy-pants event sure to be filled to the rim with rich octogenarian widows, you keep the goods a little covered up. It's just the polite thing to do.

BLACK-TIE OPTIONAL EVENTS

"Black tie optional" is the passive-aggressive mother of all dress codes. When someone sends you an invite that requests black tie optional, you should read this between the lines: "Men, please wear a tuxedo, but don't feel like you have to. I mean, we'd appreciate it if you would, but if you can't for whatever reason—maybe you don't own one, or maybe you can't afford to rent one—don't worry about it. We'll live. But it would be great if you wore one. Do your father and I really ask for that much? We sent you to college and this is how you repay us. Harvey, where are my pills?" Women, follow the rules for black tie.

The sauce makes me do things like spank myself in public. I wish this embarrassed me more than it does.

CREATIVE BLACK-TIE EVENTS

Is there anything more annoying than someone telling you to "be creative"? Well, one thing more annoying is the guy who's excited about wearing "this rainbow-colored bowtie and cummerbund I picked up three years ago in Key West" with his tuxedo. "Maybe I'll do it with cowboy boots! Wouldn't that be fun?" Ugh. Men, please just wear your good tux with an interesting pair of shoes or maybe a silk vest. Or better yet, stay home, take a nice bubble bath, and settle in for an evening of *When Harry Met Sally* and Ben and Jerry. Women, this is your big opportunity to pull out all the stops. Ostrich feathers, anyone?

↑ Brenda Dickson reference!

Jen thought this photo was disrespectful and made me swear not to use it. I had my fingers crossed.

FUNERAL

The point of a funeral is that someone is dead. And even though you might think the dead person went to a happy place, you should not appear to be happy for him or her. So at a funeral it's best to hide any signs of joy. That means dressing in dark colors like black, navy, or charcoal gray and not showing too much skin. If you want to be happy on the inside, don't wear any underwear.

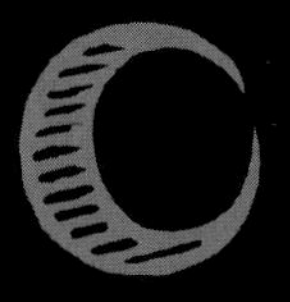

DAY TO EVENING

Taking a look from day to evening is simple. First, you remove some stuff. Then, you add some stuff.

LOOK #1: **Pencil skirt suit with silk blouse**
REMOVE: *Sensible shoe and jacket*
ADD: *Sexy heel and big jewelry*

LOOK #2: **Sheath dress**
REMOVE: *Sensible shoe and bobby pins*
ADD: *A metallic clutch and five-inch heels*

LOOK #3: **Jeans and a jacket**

Think Like a Frenchie ~ Bathe like a Yankee

The French are a complex people. They're snotty, so you want to hate them, but you can't because they're fabulous. Deep down, you suspect that they hate Americans, yet they gave us French fries and the Statue of Liberty, two presents that I, for one, don't want to return for store credit. So it is with mixed emotions that I present to you some fantastic advice I gleaned from my travels to *La France*. (That's French for France.)

See, I was working in Paris for a week back in 2000 or something. I was a magazine editor attending runway shows, but that's beside the point. On my first day of work, I noticed that everyone was perfectly dressed—in clothes that seemed custom made—and they were accessorized to the nines, or *neufs*, as they say over there. I wondered, "How am I going to compete with these people? They're so fabulous. I'll have to go shopping for a new ensemble every day!"

You can imagine how distraught I was; I had been planning to spend all my money on wine and *croissant*. (That's French for croissants.) But I did go shopping, for new shoes, sweaters, jackets, etc. Then, by the time Friday rolled around, I noticed something very weird: People were wearing the same outfits they wore on Monday!

I had never witnessed anything like it. It seemed the people of this strange, foreign land cared more about quality than about quantity. How un-American! They actually paid more money for clothes that fit them well and wore them more often. They didn't care if someone else from the office saw them in the same outfit twice in the same week. Mind-boggling.

Then I realized: That's where the smell is coming from. There's no way in hell everyone had time to dry-clean their clothes so quickly. This must be what *human beings* smell like.

Then I had another realization: I have absolutely no desire to smell like a human being. BUT . . . I do like this quality over quantity thing. I think I'll spread the word.

And so my advice is this: Think like a Frenchie, bathe like a Yankee. That is, combine the French love of quality and the American obsession with eradicating one's natural odor, and you are well on your way to true, sanitary fabulousness.

VIVE L'ANTIPERSPIRANT!

JUST YOUR AVERAGE DAY IN THE LIFE OF ME

Yesterday, I had lunch with my close personal friend, Madonna, at Balthazar. We each drank a bottle of Sancerre. And as I was walking home through SoHo, I had to use the loo, but I was stopped by so many strangers asking me questions! It's a good thing I had my camera phone with me so I could document the experience. Otherwise, you'd never believe me!

Clinton, you're just so cute! I've been wondering if you could answer a question for me. Can I wear white after Labor Day? You see, when I was a girl, we couldn't. But now all the pretty little things seem to be doing it.

ME: Hi, ma'am. I'm in a little bit of a rush, but yes, you can wear white any time you feel like it, as long as it's practical and done with a sense of purpose. For example, you wouldn't wear white open-toe shoes during a snowstorm in NYC. But, you might wear a pair of white pants to a New Year's Eve party in Miami. I even like the idea of white as a "pop" of color, or noncolor, if you will, any time of year, like carrying a white patent leather clutch with a black evening coat. Have a nice day! Gotta run!

Hey, kid, I recognize you from the boob tube. You do a program on style. I've got one for you: Should my belt match my shoes?

ME: Yes, sir, that's me. Now's not the best time to talk, but yeah, your belt should match your shoes, at least when you're dressed up. But if you're wearing jeans or something, your belt and shoes don't have to match exactly. They could be different shades of brown, for example. Or your shoes could be brown and you could even wear a green belt if you wanted to. I hope that helps! Bye!

Stop right there, sonny. I need a hand crossing the street. Wait a cotton-pickin' minute! You're Clinton Kelly! Oh, I've got a burning question that's been making me crazier than Sharon Stone. Should my bag match my shoes?

ME: Oh, dear lord, I have to tinkle. Your bag does not have to match your shoes. In fact, matching your shoes and bag is the best way to look dated and matronly. Carry a brown bag with red shoes. Or a red bag with brown shoes. Or a black bag with gold shoes. Or a gold bag with burgundy shoes. Do you catch my drift? Mix it up, lady! Ciao!

Hey, dude. Are my socks supposed to match my pants or my shoes? Have you seen my shoes?

ME: Well, there's a pair in the alley next to the SoHo Grand. I don't know if they're yours or not. In any case, I don't have time to talk right now. Your socks should match your trousers. Isn't that easy to remember? [I start to run off but return forthwith.] Wait, I should say that if you're wearing jeans, you don't have to wear blue socks. Just match your shoes. Sorry to confuse you. By the way, I think a homeless guy just stole your kicks. Loved you in *Failure to Launch*!

Should my belt, briefcase, watchband, and shoes match? Tell me now before I kill you.

ME: Wow, man, life is too damn short to get so worked up over matching your accessories. Think about all the children who are starving in China. You just worry about matching your shoes to your belt, especially when you're wearing a nice suit like this one. If your belt and shoes are black and your briefcase and watch are brown, nobody's going to blindfold you, put your back to a brick wall, and shoot you in the head. It's all good, as we say here in America. But if you did want to match them all, I'm sure you would look real nice.

SHOES!

YOU WILL **NEVER** BE **FABULOUS** WITHOUT **FABULOUS** FOOTWEAR.

That's because shoes set the tone for an outfit. Wear a chunky, clunky shoe and you look chunky and clunky. Wear a fabulous shoe and you are fabulous.
It's that simple.

How does one recognize a fabulous pair of shoes? It's difficult to explain exactly. For me, it's instinctual and very visceral. When I see a fabulous pair of shoes, a little shiver of happiness runs through me, kind of like that first second after you snort a crushed-up baby aspirin.

If you do not possess the innate ability to recognize fabulous footwear, you may be able to acquire it. The process is a little like that the Symbionese Liberation Army did to Patty Hearst. Here's what I want you to do:

These two pages contain photos of fabulous shoes. Go into a private room and look at them while engaging in some activity you enjoy for at least 15 minutes. Perhaps you can eat some chocolate, or soak your feet in a warm bath, or sniff the dirty T-shirt your gardener accidentally left in the driveway last week, ya perv. This will help your brain equate fabulousness with pleasure.

Do not turn the page!

On the next page are photographs of hideous, tacky, despicable shoes.

I want you to look at these shoes while engaging in some kind of unpleasant behavior. If you have an old Bjork CD lying around, now would be a good time to pull it out. By tomorrow you will be ready to rob a bank. I mean, by tomorrow you will recognize fabulous footwear!

Didn't I tell you they were nasty? I'm sorry to even make you look at them. But to know fabulousness, you must also know its enemy: doo-doo.

I cannot stress enough the importance of your footwear. From the ankles up you could be dressed like Coco Chanel, but with any of these on your feet, your style quotient will never be higher than that of the guy who runs the Tilt-A-Whirl.

And don't even think about giving me some spiel about "comfort." There are plenty of comfortable shoes that don't look this revolting. A few things to keep in mind:

---

1. **You can have shoes stretched by any cobbler. It makes a huge difference if they're too tight in one place, say, the toe box.**
2. **Gel pads are a girl's best friend.**
3. **Many designers now do comfort lines that are completely chic.**
4. **Wear a heel around the house a few times before wearing it out for the first time.**
5. **I never said you have to wear heels every day. The world is full of cute flats.**
6. **The commuter shoe got a bad rap, thanks to Staten Island executive assistants in the '80s. Wear a flat shoe or boot (not a *Working Girl*–style high top) to the office, then change in the ladies' room.**

And one more thing: Sometimes comfort doesn't matter. When a shoe is freakin' fabulous, it may be worth a subsequent day of misery. Soak in Epsom salts and take comfort in the fact that you're better than everyone else.

I'M SENSING A PATTERN HERE

It amazes me how many people get all wigged out over mixing patterns. To me, this is as easy as breathing. But you're not me. But maybe you're great at bowling, which I can't seem to do for the life of me. But then again, I have no desire to bowl. I'm sure that if I put my mind to it, I could be a professional bowler. It's this kind of mind-set that contributes to my fabulousness.

In any case, here's how to mix patterns.

NO PATTERNS: *Any two solids technically "go together," although some go better than others.*

ONESIES: *A single pattern can be mixed with a solid if:*

a) *That solid is a color found in the pattern*

b) *The pattern is in neutral colors*

c) *The solid is a neutral*

TWOSIES: *Two patterns can be combined if:*

a) *They have a similar color palette*

b) *One is subtle, like a pinstripe, and the other is bold*

c) *Both are subtle*

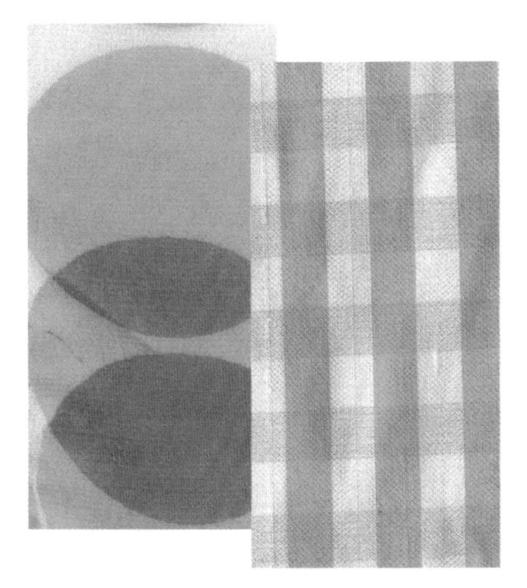

THREESIES: *Three patterns can be combined if:*

a) *Two are subtle and one is bold and they contain the same color palette*

b) *Two are bold and one is subtle and one of the bold ones is a neutral*

FOURSIES: *Four patterns can be combined if:*

Two are subtle and two are bold, but only if one of the bold patterns is used in moderation and at least one of the patterns is a neutral. Confused? To be honest with you, so am I, a little. I mean, some concepts are more difficult to explain than to do. This is Olympics-level pattern mixing, and it either comes to you easily or it doesn't. If it's not your thing, fret not. You can always try out for the archery team.

Congratulations!

You now know how to dress fabulously and are only six chapters away from being Freakin' Fabulous!

HOW TO
SPEAK

I'll be the first one to admit that using proper English can make you sound stuck-up, prissy, and out of touch with modern life, but that's no reason not to be completely familiar with the rules of grammar. There will be times you'll find yourself surrounded by stuck-up, prissy, out-of-touch types, and believe me, you don't want to give them the satisfaction of feeling superior to you because you used the word *whom* incorrectly. Fashizzle!

You might be asking yourself what gives me the right to tell you how to speak. The answer is simple: 40 grand, roughly how much I spent on my master's degree in journalism. So, suck on that.

Let's begin with the difference between *I* and *me*, *he* and *him*, *she* and *her*, *we* and *us*, and *they* and *them*.

I, HE, SHE, WE, AND **THEY** ARE SUBJECTS.
THE SUBJECT OF A SENTENCE PERFORMS THE ACTION.

I went to the liquor store and bought a nice bottle of gin.

He asked if his girlfriend could have a sip.

She drank all my liquor.

We got into a fight.

They can rot in hell for all I care.

ME, HIM, HER, US, AND **THEM** ARE OBJECTS. THE OBJECT OF A SENTENCE OR PREPOSITION RECEIVES THE ACTION.

Give that bottle to ***me.***

Don't give it to ***him*** . . .

. . . and especially not to ***her.***

Now there's less gin for ***us.***

Wow, I ***really*** don't like ***them.***

Yes, I know this is pretty basic, the kind of stuff you learn in junior high, especially the hard truth about whom to let drink your gin. But it can get tricky when you start mixing things up.

DON'T SAY:

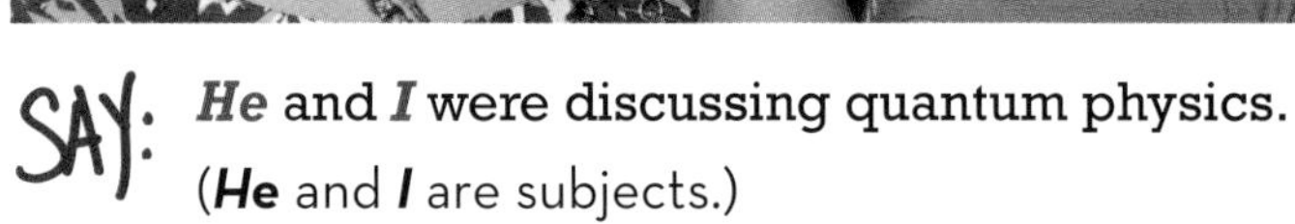

SAY: ***He*** **and** ***I*** **were discussing quantum physics.**
(***He*** and ***I*** are subjects.)

DON'T SAY:

SAY: ***She*** **and** ***her*** **mother are dating the same guy.**
(***She*** is a subject. ***Her*** is used as a possessive here.)

SAY: The clap was passed between ***him*** and ***me***.
(***Him*** and ***me*** are objects of the preposition *between*.)

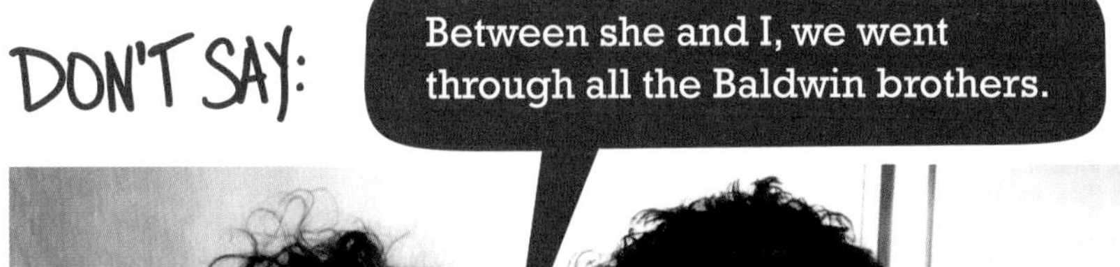

Between her and me, we went through all the Baldwin brothers.
(***Her*** and ***me*** are objects of the preposition *between*.)

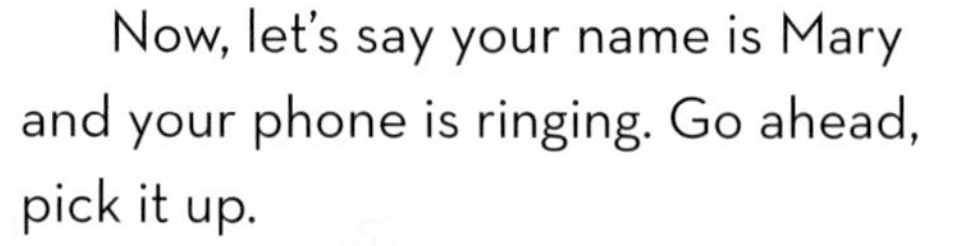

Now, let's say your name is Mary and your phone is ringing. Go ahead, pick it up.

The person on the other end asks, "Is Mary there?"

You have a few options, one of which is to answer, "Depends on who's asking." This is the option most frequently chosen by people avoiding collection agencies. If your credit is in good standing, you may answer, "This is she."

Or, if you're male, "This is he." If you are a trannie, you may say, "This is he-she."

That's because the verb *is* is a form to the verb *to be*, which requires the use of the *subject* pronoun.

Some examples:

Is that the boy who gave you a wedgie?

That is *he*.

Is that the woman who keyed your car?

That is *she*.

Are those the flowers you sent yourself so the new guy you're dating doesn't realize just how desperate you are?

Those are *they*, Mom.

When following this rule, however, you should beware of sounding like a pretentious freak. If someone asks, "Are you Mary?" you don't have to answer "That is I." You would be correct in doing so, but you'll also sound like a character from a Merchant-Ivory movie. Just say, "That's me" and get on with it. Such usage has become acceptable in modern times.

WHO AND WHOM

WHO IS A SUBJECT PRONOUN AND
WHOM IS AN OBJECT PRONOUN.

The following sentences are all correct.

Who drank my gin?
(***Who*** is the subject; ***drank*** is the verb.)

You gave my gin ***to whom***?
(***To*** is a preposition; ***whom*** is the object.)

That's the guy ***who drinks*** too much gin.
(***Who*** is the subject; ***drinks*** is the verb.)

That's the guy ***whom*** I yelled ***at*** for drinking all my gin.
(Here you might have to juggle a few words around to figure out whether to use who or whom. Forget "***that's the guy***" is even part of the sentence.) I yelled at whom for drinking all my gin. (***At*** is the preposition; ***whom*** is the object. Of course, you could just cheat by saying, "***That's the guy I yelled at for drinking all my gin***.")

May I ask who is calling?
(***Who*** is the subject; ***is*** is the verb.)

Whom would you like to speak to?
(***To*** is a preposition; ***whom*** is its object.)

Give the leftover gin to whomever.
(***To*** is the preposition; ***whomever*** is the object.)

Give the leftover gin to whoever wants it.
(***Whoever*** is the subject; ***wants*** is the verb.)

DANGLING MODIFIERS

These drive me nuts. If you're going to use an introductory clause, make sure it's referring to the subject of the sentence.

"Running to answer the door, my martini splashed all over the hand-knotted silk rug."

Wrong, wrong and WRONG!

This sentence implies that the martini is the one running to answer the door, which probably didn't happen, unless you were dropping acid at the time. Instead say, "Running to answer the door, *I* splashed my martini all over the rug." Or construct the sentence differently: "I splashed my martini all over the rug while I was running to answer the door. I guess I was excited about the prospect of the UPS guy seeing me in my new hot pants."

Let's do some more. These are fun!

> "Flying from Paris to New York, the Mile-High Club gained two more members."

NOPE! This sentence implies that the Mile-High Club was flying from Paris to New York. I can absolutely tell you that this did NOT happen, because the president of the MHC would have called me personally to invite me on the trip, which he didn't. Instead, you could say, "Flying from Paris to New York, *we* joined the Mile-High Club." Of course, you could always construct the sentence differently: "The Mile-High Club gained two more members while we flew from Paris to New York. Sometimes being a cliché is fun!"

Here's another, slightly trickier one:

> "Considering her ineptitude, Francine shouldn't be allowed anywhere near the kitchen."

This sentence implies that Francine was considering her own ineptitude. Was she? If so, the sentence should probably read something like, "Considering her ineptitude, Francine voluntarily barred herself from my kitchen." Got it? You can just picture Francine standing there, looking kind of dumb, thinking about how useless she would be. On some level this gives me some respect for Francine because I don't want anyone helping me in the kitchen who doesn't know a slotted spoon from a pasta fork.

But back to the original sentence . . . It's more likely that we were talking about Francine behind her back. In that case, we could say, "Considering her ineptitude, we should keep Francine as far away from the kitchen as possible." See, in this last example, *we* are the ones doing the considering.

You know, the more I think about it, the less I like Francine. She borrowed 20 bucks from me last month and never paid me back.

LAY OR LIE?

Here's a funny story:

My friend Sarah had been sending her dog to an obedience trainer for a couple of weeks, but the dog, whom we'll call Happy, hadn't been showing too many signs of progress. One day, while Happy was at the trainer's studio, Sarah decided to run a few errands. About 3:00 that afternoon, she called me from the U.S. Immigration Office, saying she was stuck in a really long queue (she's British), and asked me to pick up Happy. She was a fairly new friend at the time, so she didn't know about the unspoken agreement I have with all my friends: You don't ask me for favors and I won't ask you. I find that life is much less complicated this way.

Anyhow, I obliged—this one time—and headed to pick up the dog. When I arrived, I checked in with the receptionist, who knew to expect me, and listened to the last bit of the trainer's lesson. He was giving Happy treats and telling the dog to "lay down."

I was horrified!

When the trainer, whose name I don't even know, brought Happy to the waiting area, I couldn't keep myself from speaking up.

"Hi," I said. "I'm Clinton. I'm here to pick up Happy. His mom's stuck at the Immigration Office."

The trainer replied, "I hope everything's all right."

"Everything's cool, but I was wondering if I could give you some professional advice."

He looked perplexed. "Me? Yeah, I guess so."

"I noticed you told Happy to lay down," I said, "when the correct word is *lie* down. I think this could be part of the reason Happy isn't doing so well at home. See, his mother, my friend Sarah, is a stickler for proper English, and I'm sure she's telling Happy to lie down. The dog is probably very confused."

I had expected an awkward pause, but this one lasted longer than I thought appropriate. Then, the trainer, a tall man, leaned in toward me and whispered in my ear, "Why don't you go f#$% yourself."

"I'll take that under advisement," I said. "Let's go, Happy."

I don't speak to Sarah anymore. She just stopped calling. I don't care because

I'm very busy and the British require a lot of attention. Anyway, the moral of this story is, I guess, that proper grammar is important even for our four-legged friends. And children too!

You must remember the following:

LAY MEANS TO **PLACE SOMETHING.**

For example: You lay a Xanax on your lover's pillow before bed.

LIE MEANS TO **RECLINE.**

You lie around the house all day because you're hungover.

The past tense is where some people get screwed up.

THE PAST TENSE OF **LAY** (TO PLACE) IS **LAID**.

Last night, someone laid a Xanax on my pillow. How thoughtful.

THE PAST TENSE OF **LIE** (TO RECLINE) IS **LAY**.

Yesterday, you lay around the house all day because you're a lazy, good-for-nothing skank.

THE PAST PARTICIPLE OF LAY (TO PLACE) IS **LAID**. *Tricky!*

I have laid a Xanax on your pillow every night for the last three months and you've never even thanked me.

THE PAST PARTICIPLE OF LIE (TO RECLINE) IS **LAIN**.

You have lain around this house every day for the past three months. Remind me why I stay with you? Oh, yes, the children need a role model.

OK, folks, it's time for a quiz! Fill in the blanks below with the correct form of lay or lie. (Answers are below.)

1. "Oh, sweetie, you look tired. Why don't you .... down and take a nap. I promise I won't seduce the UPS man again while you're asleep."

2. "Your mama may have .... your clothes out for you every night, but I'm not going to. This is an orphanage, not the Ritz-Carlton."

3. "Do me a favor, will ya? Take that piece of raw bacon and .... it on the cutting board. I'm making rumaki!" (To learn how to make rumaki, see page 170!)

4. "How did she get that job? She .... on her back for it. See, she's a model and the casting director for the mattress ad campaign wanted to see how she'd photograph from above."

5. "Those dead bodies have .... in the morgue for three days now. By the way, this place stinks."

6. "I hate the way you .... your hands on me last night. It really was the worst massage I ever had."

7. "If a man you're dating buys you dinner three times, he expects to get ...."

ANSWERS: *1. lie; 2. laid; 3. lay; 4. lay; 5. lain; 6. laid; 7. a firm handshake and a sincere thank-you at the end of the evening.*

THE SUBJUNCTIVE MOOD

I really don't want to make this grammar stuff too complicated, so I'm just going to explain a little about the subjunctive mood. You can use it when you're stating a wish.

For example:

INCORRECT: I wish I was a princess.

CORRECT: I wish I ***were*** a princess.

(Just so you know, I do not wish I were a princess.)

INCORRECT: I wish he was better in bed.

CORRECT: I wish he ***were*** better in bed.

You can also use the subjunctive when you're stating something contrary to fact.

INCORRECT: If she wasn't a hoochie mama, she'd get taken out to dinner more frequently.

CORRECT: If she ***weren't*** a hoochie mama, she'd get taken out to dinner more frequently.

INCORRECT: If he was good-looking, I wouldn't have to picture Chris Noth.

CORRECT: If he ***were*** good-looking, I wouldn't have to picture Chris Noth.

You get it now, right?

THAT VS. WHO

Adjective clauses and relative pronouns . . . blah, blah, blah. Here's what you need to know:

"WHO" REFERS TO PEOPLE.
"THAT" REFERS TO OBJECTS AND ANIMALS AND SOMETIMES PEOPLE.

There's the girl ***who*** stole your Christian LouBoutin shoes.

There's the car ***that*** ran over your cashmere sweater.

There's the monkey ***that*** ripped your pants.

Wow, you're having a crappy day.

THAT OR WHICH?

When deciding whether to use "that" or "which," I like to mentally insert the phrase "by the way" into the sentence. If it fits, use "which." I'll explain:

I have a recipe for roasted fennel ***that*** will blow your mind.

The recipe, ***which*** I received from my grandmother, calls for lots of butter.

(See, I could say, "The recipe, which I received from my grandmother, by the way, calls for lots of butter." I'm sort of throwing the grandmother thing in there as an aside. It's not essential to the thought of the sentence.)

More:

I have done things ***that*** I'm not proud of.

Robbing that bank, ***which*** employed a lot of hot tellers, was probably a mistake.

She has clothes ***that*** are very expensive.

Her boobs, ***which*** are fake as fake can be, are 38Ds.

He wears cologne *that* smells like a night at the Roxbury.

ANYONE AND EVERYONE AND HIS OR HER VS. THEIR

"Anyone" and "everyone" are singular nouns, so they take singular forms of verbs and pronouns.

INCORRECT: Anyone can find ***themselves*** in credit card debt.
(***Themselves*** is plural.)

CORRECT: Anyone can find ***himself*** in credit card debt.
(Or if you were referring to a woman, ***herself***.)

INCORRECT: Could everyone please take ***their*** seats?

CORRECT: Could everyone please take ***his or her*** seat?

INCORRECT: Does anyone actually lose ***their*** virginity at the prom?

CORRECT: Does anyone actually lose ***his or her*** virginity at the prom? God knows I didn't.

MORE THAN VS. OVER

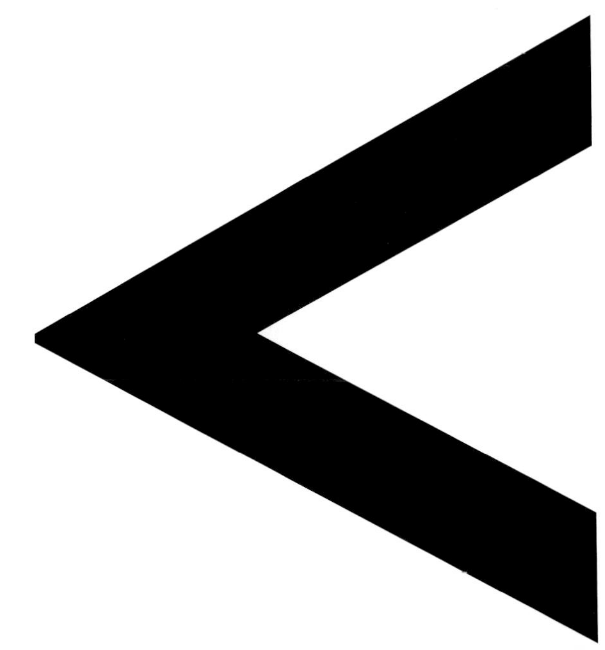

"Over" has become synonymous with "more than," which drives some grammarians crazy.

I must have told him ***over*** a thousand times not to wear those cutoff jean shorts.

Instead say:

I must have told him ***more than*** a thousand times not to wear those shorts. They make his legs look fat.

FEWER VS. LESS

I'm almost hesitant to explain the difference between "fewer" and "less" to people who don't already know it. You see, from this moment forward, not a day will pass without you noticing someone using the words incorrectly. You will want to correct him (or her), but I suggest you don't.

"FEWER" SHOULD BE USED WHEN DESCRIBING THINGS YOU CAN ACTUALLY COUNT. USE **"LESS"** OR **"LESS THAN"** FOR MORE AMBIGUOUS OR GENERAL CONCEPTS.

I have ***fewer*** grains of sand in my hand than you do.

You have ***less*** sand in your hair than I do.
(You can count grains of sand, but you can't count sand in general.)

I have ***less*** money than Tyra.

I bet I have ***fewer*** dollars in my wallet than she does right now.
(You can count actual pieces of money, but "money" is a general concept.)

You have had ***less*** sex than I.

You have had ***fewer*** sexual partners than I.
(You can count actual people having sex, but not "sex" itself. And, by the way, I'm not bragging.)

FURTHER VS. FARTHER

WHEN REFERRING TO PHYSICAL DISTANCE, USE "**FARTHER**." WHEN YOU'RE REFERRING TO TIME, AMOUNT, OR ABSTRACT IDEAS, USE "**FURTHER**."

I can't walk any ***farther*** in these five-inch heels.

I don't want to discuss your cross-dressing any ***further***.

Let me know about any ***further*** developments regarding that rash.

Mine extends ***farther*** down my leg.

CONTINUAL VS. CONTINUOUS

"**CONTINUAL**" REFERS TO SOMETHING THAT IS REPEATED OVER AND OVER. "**CONTINUOUS**" REFERS TO SOMETHING UNBROKEN.

Her ***continual*** repetition of the word "like" made me want to gag.

It's amazing that she can speak ***continuously*** for 20 minutes without giving anyone else a chance.

Some more examples:

Someone can have a ***continuous*** stretch of bad relationships by ***continually*** choosing the wrong guy.

She's ***continually*** late for work.

He has been ***continuously*** frustrated.

IMPLY VS. INFER

When you imply something, you're the one delivering the information, perhaps slyly. When you infer something, you've put two and two together and have come to a conclusion.

I *implied* that she was a bad mother because I told her she shouldn't smoke while breast-feeding.

When she *inferred* that I was judging her, she burned me with her cigarette.

BETWEEN VS. AMONG

Use "between" when referring to two people. Use "among" when referring to three or more.

TRY TO

Just a little pet peeve of mine:

When someone asks you to stop by their apartment, don't say you'll "try and" come. Say you'll "try *to*" come.

Could you try *to* find that lost earring?

She'll try *to* make potato salad.

I'll try *to* be more concerned about your damn feelings, but don't count on it.

COULD HAVE, SHOULD HAVE, WOULD HAVE

I'm going off-topic for a minute here because this is my book and I feel like it. Do yourself a favor and banish the words *coulda*, *shoulda*, and *woulda* from your vocabulary—especially when referring to yourself. First, they don't actually exist in the English language, and second, they make you sound like a complete and total LOSER and a BORE.

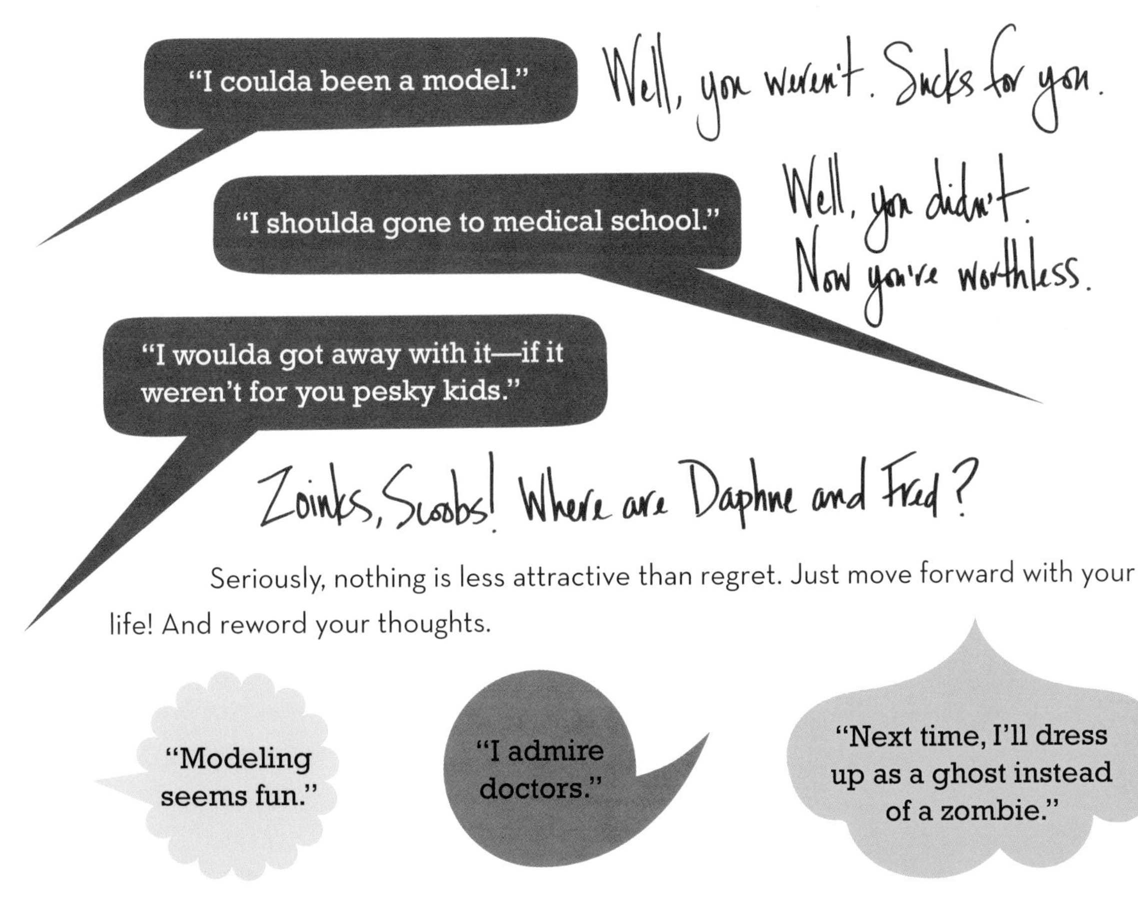

Seriously, nothing is less attractive than regret. Just move forward with your life! And reword your thoughts.

Now, if you find that you must use the phrase "could have" (or its siblings), please realize that it does indeed consist of two words, "could" and "have." Most people contract them into "could've," which is acceptable in conversation and informal writing. However, it is absolutely *beyond* unacceptable to write "could of." Aaaaaack! "She could of married him." Oh, I could rip my own hair out right now just thinking about it.

THE REASON IS BECAUSE

Don't use this construction. The reason isn't because of anything.

CORRECT: The reason I am late is ***that*** I was attacked by a deranged Chihuahua.

OR I am late because I was attacked by a deranged Chihuahua. Don't laugh. I needed three stitches and a tetanus shot!

LITERALLY

I have a confession: I think it's fun to intentionally misuse the word "literally" when speaking to friends because it creates a sense of drama and interesting imagery.

Me, on the phone to my sister: "Omigod, when I told that woman on my show that she looked like the illegitimate child of Morticia Addams and Pee-Wee Herman, her head literally spun around, flew off her shoulders, and hit a camera guy in the solar plexus."

We both know this didn't actually happen, but it's thrilling to imagine.

It's not so cute when you're on a job interview and you tell the human resources department that your former boss was "literally a douche bag."

RANDOM STUFF

A few more pet peeves of mine:

INTENSIVE PURPOSES

Occasionally, I'll hear someone use the phrase "for all intensive purposes." I agree, it does sound very official, like something Harrison Ford would say in a spy movie: "Yes, Mr. President, we've received detailed information from our Intensive Purposes department that Luxembourg is about to declare war on the United States."

The actual phrase, however, is "for all *intents and* purposes." As in "For all intents and purposes, let's just forget this ever happened when we see each other at work tomorrow."

THERE'S

Just so you know, I commit this next infraction more than I feel comfortable admitting.

"There's" is a contraction of "there" and "is" and therefore should be used only as substitution for "there is." For example, I know that the following two sentences are correct:

"There's bean dip in the fridge if you're hungry."

"There's nothing any shrink can do about your personality disorder."

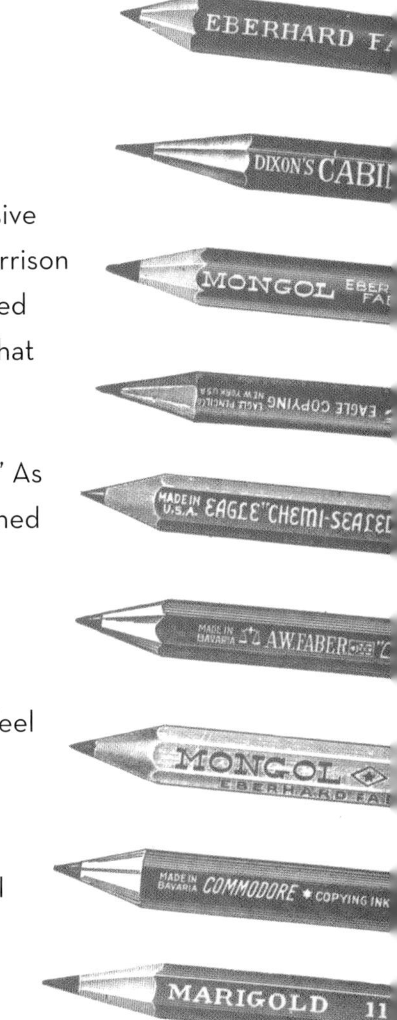

Editing this book. I look like I'm on crack. I'm not.

But sometimes I will hear myself utter a sentence like:

"There's a hundred things wrong with your outfit."

Yikes! *Did I just say that? How gauche. I know it's incorrect, but it already came out of my mouth! What do I do? I'll ignore it and hope nobody noticed. Deep down I know that people are judging me. I will break myself of this bad habit.*

CORRECT: **"There are a hundred things wrong with your outfit."**

OR **"There're a hundred things wrong with your outfit."**

Yes, I'm human. Go ahead and feel superior if you want. By the way, I hate your shoes.

ANYWAYS

There's no such word. Drop the *s*.

"Anyway, as I was saying, she's a slut."

SUPPOSABLY

I don't know where this came from, but I hear it all too frequently. The word is *supposedly*, people. With a *d*, not a *b*.

"Supposedly, when the cops found him, he was wearing women's underwear."

I's

This one is a doozie. Sometimes people think they're being all fancy because they're using the word "I" instead of "me," but they'll forget that the possessive form of "I" is "my."

Here's where you'll hear it:

"Just because we started dancing with her boyfriend, Donna got all up in Jenny and *I's* face."

Ugh. There is no such word as I's! It's *my* face!

"Donna got all up in Jenny's and my face."

Congratulations!

You now know how to speak fabulously and are now five chapters away from being FREAKIN' FABULOUS!

FF

HOW TO
BEHAVE

Many people are turned off by the topics of manners and etiquette because they conjure images of old biddies wearing their hair in tight buns, drinking tea, and discussing the infrequency of their bowel movements.

I'd like to change that perception. The modern world is a casual one, and that's great on so many levels. But an unfortunate consequence of the 21st-century lifestyle is an all-too-common lack of respect for one's fellow citizens and a general shortage of civility. Life moves fast. Communication is impersonal. And for some reason, we reward bad behavior with magazine covers and television coverage. I don't know about you, but I think it's pretty sad that so many starlets have discovered that flashing their junk while exiting a vehicle is the best PR. Get some freakin' class!

Being fabulous means knowing how to behave in every situation, whether that's a good old-fashioned bar fight or a private dinner at the White House. For now, I'll assume you know how to block a right hook delivered by a drunken Irish guy and that you're not exactly Secretary of State material. So I'll focus on a few of the situations you might encounter on a day-to-day basis, like how to eat soup or what's appropriate to bring to a party or who should enter a revolving door first.

I hope it helps.

DINING OUT

When you're at home alone on the couch eating Chinese takeout, do whatever it takes to get that General Tso's chicken into your mouth—use chopsticks, your fingers, graze directly from the bowl. But when you're dining in a restaurant or at a private dinner party, certain "rules" apply. For some people, these may seem fairly basic, but I've witnessed too many public faux pas to think they're universal.

YOUR NAPKIN

Remove your napkin from the table as soon as you've been seated and place it in your lap, preferably folded in half, with the fold toward you. If getting it into that shape and position would be awkward, don't make a big deal about doing so; you don't have to shake it out with a flourish like a maître d' in a bad movie and refold it properly.

The napkin should stay on your lap throughout the entire meal and return to the table only when you are exiting the table and on your way out of the room. Should you need to excuse yourself from the table at any time, lay the napkin on the *seat* of your chair, not the back.

Yes, I know that in many restaurants, servers will refold your napkin and return it to the table, but this is wrong and, quite frankly, gross. Nobody at your table wants to see a napkin smeared with lipstick and puttanesca.

BREAD AND BUTTER

Don't dive into the bread basket without first offering some to your dining companions. When everyone else has accepted or declined, take a piece for yourself along with some butter, which you should place on your bread plate using your butter knife.

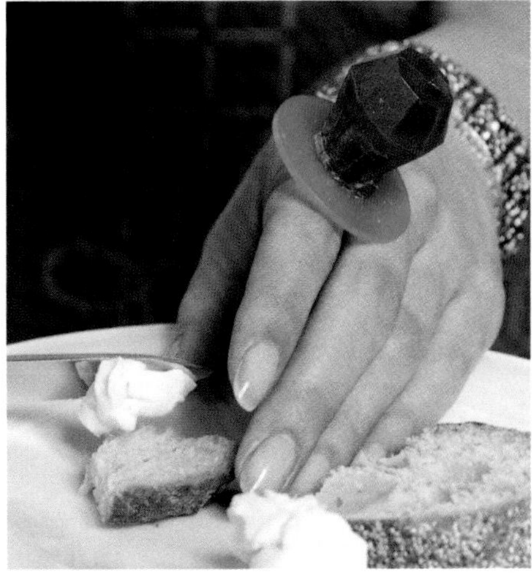

Don't butter the entire roll or slice of bread at once. Break off a small piece of bread, one or two bites' worth, and butter as you go. And keep the bread on the plate while buttering it. Don't hold it in the air or in the palm of your hand, like you would smear mayo on a slice of rye. The butter knife should rest fully on your butter plate throughout dinner, not touching the table at all.

If olive oil has been provided for dipping, you may either pour or spoon some onto your own butter plate or dip from a communal bowl. If the latter is the best option, be sure to break your bread into bite-size pieces before dipping. Never dip any piece of bread that has already touched your mouth; that's how cooties are transmitted.

YOU MAY BEGIN

I don't care if you haven't eaten in three days—don't start eating until everyone at your table has been served!

Sometimes a restaurant will keep one person waiting for his or her meal, which is one of the biggest screw-ups the kitchen and/or server can make because it puts everyone in an awkward position. We've all been there. The person waiting to be served may say, "Please, everyone, eat before your food gets cold." I think it best to offhandedly assure the unserved that waiting is really no bother. If he or she becomes insistent, just begin eating slowly and keep the conversation going, avoiding statements like, "Whew, I thought I was going to starve to death for a minute there."

SALT AND PEPPER

Don't salt your food before tasting it. Doing so implies that the preparer doesn't know how to properly season a dish. This might not insult a chef who can't see you, but it very well might piss off the host of a private dinner party who spent three hours slaving away over an osso bucco for your ungrateful ass. OK, then.

Another thing to keep in mind about the S&P is that they should be treated as a codependent couple—they do not like to be separated. If someone asks for one, pass him both.

SAUCES

If a sauce of some kind is served on the side—hollandaise, béarnaise, bordelaise, A1—don't pour it directly onto your food. Pour a little pool on the side of your plate and dip your food (using a fork!) into it as you go. Replenish the pool as necessary.

REACHING

If an item is farther than arm's length away (while you're sitting upright in your chair), ask someone to pass it to you. And say please, you heathen.

ELBOWS

Contrary to popular belief, your elbows are indeed allowed to touch the table during dinner. It's only natural to put one or two on the table while engaging in conversation. However, once food is served, keep your elbows down and to your sides.

HOW TO HOLD A WINEGLASS

Wines and Champagne (or other sparkling wines) are meant to be drunk at the temperature they are served. That's why restaurants lock wines in cellars and chill them in coolers. When you hold a glass by its bowl, your body temperature warms the wine. So don't. Hold the glass by the stem; that's why it's there. You'll also avoid all those greasy fingerprints and smudges. (By the way, you've probably noticed that a brandy snifter doesn't have much of a stem. That's because liquors served in snifters are meant to be warmed by the hand.)

HOLDING THE FLATWARE

There are two acceptable styles of dining in the United States: Continental and American. (Continental refers to the continent of Europe, by the way.) I find Continental style to make a little more sense because you don't have to keep passing the fork back and forth from hand to hand, but use whichever style you prefer.

American-style dining

American-style resting flatware

American-style ending flatware

AMERICAN STYLE

Hold the fork in your left hand, tines facing down, with your index finger positioned under the base of the fork.

Hold the knife in your right hand, blade facing down, with your index finger positioned where the handle and blade meet.

Your forearms should be off the table and your elbows to your sides.

Insert the fork into the food to keep it steady, and cut off a bite-size piece.

Place the knife on the edge of your plate.

Switch the fork to your right hand, turning the tines up, and bring to your mouth.

Return the fork to your left hand, tines down.

Chew your food, swallow, and repeat. (Don't start cutting again while you're still chewing. Remember what I said about social dining—it's not about shoveling food into your face.) Proper American style dictates that you push the food with the knife in your right hand onto the fork in your left, tines up. Place the knife down, move the fork to your right hand, and bring the food to your mouth.

CONTINENTAL STYLE

Hold the fork in your left hand, tines facing down, with your index finger positioned under the base of the fork.

Hold the knife in your right hand, blade facing down (obviously), with your index finger where the handle meets the blade.

Your forearms should be off the table and your elbows to your sides.

Insert the fork into the food to keep it steady, and cut off a bite-size piece.

You may place the knife down onto the plate or keep holding it (this is when your wrist can touch the table).

Keeping the fork in your left hand, tines facing down, bring your food to your mouth.

Chew, swallow, and repeat.

If your food does not require cutting, use the knife to push food onto the fork. In the Continental style, the tines of the fork always remain facing down.

A note to lefties: Change everything I just said about right to left and left to right.

Continental-style dining

Continental-style resting flatware

Continental-style ending flatware

RESTING FLATWARE

If you'd like to take a little break while eating your meal, think about taking "A" break. You make sort of a capital letter A with your flatware. The knife rests on the right-hand side of your plate (not leaning on the table) with the tip facing the top, blade facing in. The fork is its mirror image on the left side, with tines facing down if you're eating Continental style. They can be facing up or down if you're dining American style. By the way, you should avoid leaving the table while food is present, if at all possible.

ENDING FLATWARE

To signal to the server that you've finished your meal, place the fork and knife parallel to each other diagonally across the right-hand side of the plate. Once again, if you're following Continental style, the tines of the fork will probably face down and when following American style, the fork tines will probably be facing up. But neither is set in stone. It's that parallel parking that's important.

Never "help" your server by stacking up your bread plate on your dinner plate—or other people's plates on yours. Yikes! Clearing plates is the server's job, and he's probably happy to do it himself.

A note about the end of your main course: An overeager server or busperson might attempt to clear plates as people finish their meals, which is incorrect and pretty rude. If you're still eating, you shouldn't be rushed, plain and simple. And you shouldn't let anyone else be rushed. When that server asks if you're finished and you see your friend Sally still chomping away, tell the server politely, "You can clear the plates when we're all finished, thank you."

And that brings me to a note about talking to your servers in a restaurant:

I worked in the restaurant industry for years, as a busboy through high school and waiting tables through college and grad school. And let me just tell you, nothing makes you look like more of a cow than treating your server as an inferior.

When dining out, say please and thank you; make eye contact; don't snap your fingers; and tip for good service. Also, keep in mind that bad food is not your waiter's fault. He didn't make it.

On the flip side, there's no reason to be your waiter's best friend. A thank you is unnecessary every time a drink is delivered or a plate is cleared. And I also think that the restaurant management should be informed of particularly bad service, but leaving a penny as a tip is passive-aggressive and makes you look like an ass.

EATING SOUP

Hold your soupspoon in your hand so that it's resting on top of your fingers and held in place with your thumb. The spoon enters the bowl from the side and you spoon away from you. To get the last of the soup onto your spoon, you may tilt the bowl away from you.

A FEW TRICKY ONES

SPAGHETTI. Basically, you can twirl it on a spoon. Or you can just twirl it on your plate until it forms a reasonable mouthful. If you've got danglers, bite them off and let them fall back to the plate. It's OK. That's how they do it in Italy. Same goes for linguine and other long pastas.

OYSTERS. If you're served oysters on the half shell during a fancy dinner, hold the shell with one hand and with the other use your shellfish fork to spear the oyster. Then dip the oyster into the sauce provided, and bring the meat, not the shell, to your mouth. Or you could dip the fork into the sauce first, adding some to the oyster while it's in the shell, then bring the sauced meat to your mouth. Same goes for clams on the half shell. However, I think missing out on the oyster's liquor (the juice left behind) is a tragedy and certainly could not fault anyone for giving the shell a quick sip. If you're dining in a seafood restaurant, go ahead and suck the oyster meat right out of its shell.

LAMB CHOPS. You may pick up a lamb chop served as a main course with your fingers if the following three criteria have been met: 1. You have removed as much meat as possible with your fork and knife; 2. What's left isn't dripping in sauce; 3. You are not at a formal affair or a very upscale dining establishment. Otherwise, just leave it on your plate. (This rule applies to a small pork chop or any other chop you could maneuver single-handedly.)

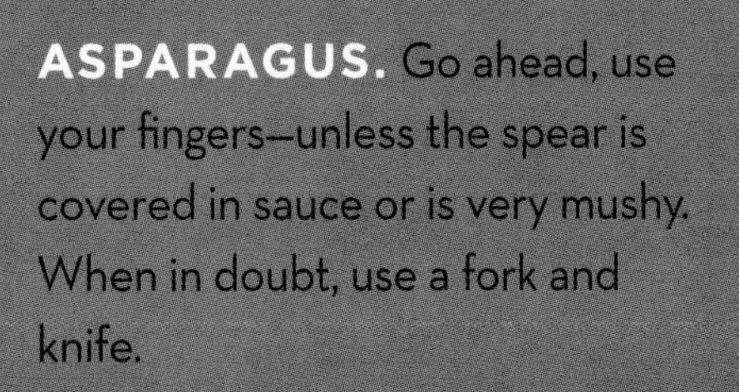

ASPARAGUS. Go ahead, use your fingers—unless the spear is covered in sauce or is very mushy. When in doubt, use a fork and knife.

SALAD. You know how moms cut up a whole plate of food for a toddler? Don't do that to your own salad. Actually, don't do it to any adult food. Cut bite-size pieces as you go. If you hate cutting salad as much as I do, opt for the chopped salad when possible.

WHOLE LOBSTER. Look, don't even order this at a nice restaurant unless you really know what you're doing. Practice on a few at home or at your local lobster shack. A really fancy-shmancy place will de-shell it for you.

KISSING

Nothing ruins a perfectly nice meal for an entire restaurant than being forced to watch the one couple so in love they can't keep their hands off each other. (And have you noticed, it's always a guy with a big gold watch and a woman who has applied her foundation with a trowel.) If you see them touch tongues, I give you permission to hurl dinner rolls at their heads. The next time you get this horned up in public, please just go have sex in the bathroom like everyone else.

LIPSTICK ET AL

I hereby pronounce you tacky if you apply lipstick, powder, mascara, nail polish, eye liner, blush, or any other cosmetic while seated at the table. Same goes for plucking your eyebrows, looking into a mirror, filing your nails, checking your teeth for poppy seeds, brushing your hair, and applying perfume. Now that I've insulted half of Orange County, let's move on.

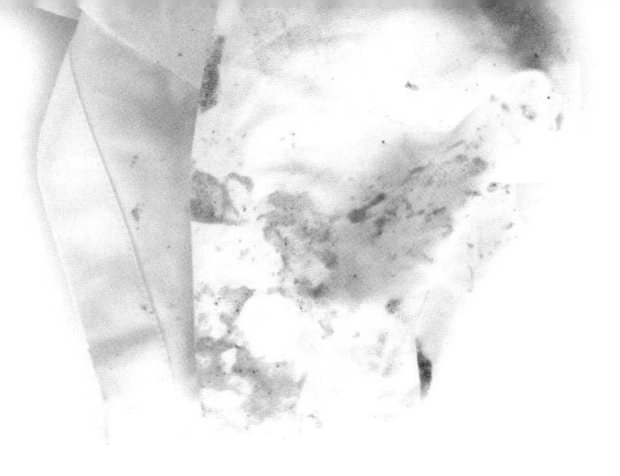

COUGHING, SNEEZING, AND BLOWING

Sometimes a cough or a sneeze can sneak up on you. If you have time to fetch a tissue or handkerchief out of your pocket or bag, do so. If not, turn your head away from the table, and cover your mouth and nose with your napkin. Do not blow your nose in your napkin. Do not blow your nose at the table at all. Excuse yourself and use the restroom.

FOOD IN YOUR TEETH

Got a little broccoli wedged between your two front choppers? For God's sake, don't use your acrylic fingernail, your fork, or the corner of your napkin to remove it. Most food stuck in your teeth can be dislodged with a gentle swabbing of the tongue—preferably your own. But if that wad is really jammed in there and you're starting to suck your own face like a deranged orangutan, leave the table with an "Excuse me, please" and dislodge it in the restroom.

FOOD IN SOMEONE ELSE'S TEETH

Let's say you notice that one of your dining companions has an out-of-place piece of food somewhere on his person. What do you do? If it's a poppy seed in the teeth, just let it go. No big whoop. On the other hand, if it's a drop of sauce on his chin or a quail leg in his beard, you should make him aware of it as discreetly as possible. If you are seated next to him, whisper softly but lightheartedly, "You've got a little something on your cheek." If you're seated across from him, you might just gesture to your own chin. If it's a booger, don't say anything or make any moves unless that bat in the cave looks like it's about to drop outta there any second.

SOMETHING NASTY!

Let's say you spot a bug in your soup or a hair on your salad that is most certainly not yours. Gross, I know. And because of the shock, your initial reaction might be to announce it to everyone at the table. But don't. Instead, just put your utensils down and try to gain the attention of the waiter. When he arrives, tell him there's a foreign object in your soup and leave it at that. He should bring you a new one as quickly as possible, which you may choose to accept or not. Should your gag reflex kick in at any time, disguise it by holding your napkin to your mouth.

DISCARDING THINGS LIKE BONES, OLIVE PITS, AND WRAPPERS

Should you encounter a bone in your fish, don't make a big deal about it, as if someone were trying to kill you. "Oh, there's a bone. I could have choked to death." I hate that. Fish have bones! Subtly extract it from your mouth and place it on the edge of your plate.

If olives are served as an appetizer, they should be served with a pit dish. If no dish is available, place your pits on your bread plate—not on the tablecloth. If olives with pits are served with your main course, place the pits on the edge of your dinner plate.

If butter is served in individually wrapped pats, leave the wrapper on your bread plate. If plastic-wrapped crackers are served, tuck any wrappers next to your bread plate.

TIPPING POINTERS

I have a general rule of fabulousness: Never tip anyone less than a buck.

I don't care if it's a bartender who poured you a soda, an Albuquerque cab driver, or the kid who delivers your Sunday paper. Two shiny quarters may have been generous back in 1952, but today they won't even buy you a cup of coffee. Many people in the service industry make less than minimum wage because they rely on tips. Hook 'em up.

With that said, I don't think it's necessary to give a dollar every time you get a venti-triple-half-caff-nonfat-sugar-free-vanilla-cappu-latte. Tip jars are optional and should be used when you've received exceptional service.

Here are some general rules of thumb:

WAITSTAFF: 15% for average service; 18% for very good; 20% for exceptional.

BARTENDERS: $1 a drink for sodas, beer, and basic drinks; $2 for more elaborate concoctions

COAT CHECK: $1 per item

HAIRSTYLIST: 15% for a good job; 20% if you love your new 'do.

MANICURIST/PEDICURIST: 15%

MASSAGE THERAPIST/ FACIALIST: 15% for a good massage; 20% for a great one

DRIVER (taxi or car service): 15% for good service; 20% if driver helped with bags, opened doors, etc.

VALET PARKING: $3 upon retrieval of your car—slip him at least $5 when handing over your car if you want to make sure your Porsche doesn't get scratched.

A NOTE ON TIPPING

Never tip anyone you're sleeping with. It makes her or him feel like a whore.

Clinton Kelly's Guide to
FREAKIN' FABULOUS BODILY FUNCTIONS

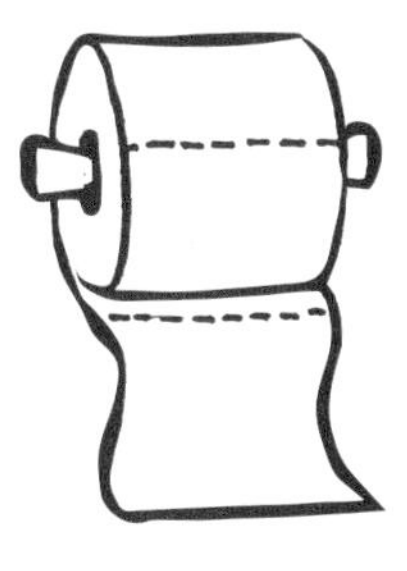

MY LEAST FAVORITE THING ABOUT BEING HUMAN IS ALL THE STUFF THAT COMES OUT OF OUR BODIES. I SHOULD PROBABLY TALK TO A SHRINK ABOUT IT, BUT I THINK IT'S PRETTY GROSS. ANYWAY, YOU MIGHT BE MORE ACCEPTING OF ALL YOUR FLUIDS AND GASSES AND SOLIDS THAN I. IF SO, GOOD FOR YOU. BUT I STILL RECOMMEND ADHERING TO THE FOLLOWING GUIDELINES.

Gas Up Above

In some countries, burping is a compliment to the chef, that you enjoyed her meal. Last time I checked, this was not one of those countries. If you have to burp, keep your mouth closed and cover it with your napkin. If one escapes, just say, "Excuse me," and don't make a big deal about it. When you say, "Oh, that pork sandwich I had for breakfast is really repeating on me!" it makes me visualize the contents of your stomach, and I really don't want to do that.

Gas Down Below

The number one rule of farting is: If you have to fart, leave the room. Don't know how to make a graceful yet brief exit? Try this line: "Excuse me while I go say a little prayer."

One Accidentally Slips Out

If it's audible, immediately break into song, preferably something patriotic, like "You're a Grand Ole Flag." If it's silent, leave the room and let whoever's left give each other dirty looks. I don't think you should ever say, "Excuse me" for farting. Let's just pretend it never happened. Oh, and never, ever fart in an elevator. That's just evil.

Numbers One and Two (a.k.a. Pee and Poo)

I can't stand it when people say things like, "I have to tinkle" or "I'm about to have a visit from the chocolate stork." I DON'T WANT TO KNOW ABOUT IT! Just go into the bathroom and do what you have to do. And if you're in someone else's house, run the water in the sink to muffle any sounds. If your eco-conscience objects to wasting water, sing "You're a Grand Ole Flag."

alison

Clinton,
Could that party have been more fun? I don't think so. I totally made out with three hot gay guys! Thanks for inviting me!
Love!
Alison

THE ST. REGIS
HOTEL

Thank you for Dinner
Your Snoring Kept me up all night!

I stole your Prada Sweater Vest.

Don't call me!!

X

Clinton—
Your generosity overwhelms me. I wish we could go on a crime spree in a small town so that we could be locked up together in a tiny cell and the sheriff's wife would feed us chicken and biscuits.
Troy

Thanks for holding my hair back while I puked — & for the pillow
XO

HWB

Clinton,
Oh my God. The Gold clutch you gave me for my birthday is beyond fierce! I'd offer to bear your Children but I doubt I could give up Xanax for 9 months. And you've seen firsthand how my own kids turned out.
Love, Kathlee[n]

THANK YOU!

Get yourself into the habit of sending thank-you cards. In this day of impersonal e-mails and mailboxes stuffed to the brim with catalogs, bills, and credit card offers, receiving an actual handwritten letter is almost as exciting as finding a note in your locker between homeroom and first period that says, "I think your argyle sweater is super cute. Wanna make out after school?" Here are some thank-you notes I've been sent by fabulous people over the years. Feel free to plagiarize if you want. They'll never find out. Half the senders are in rehab and the other half I don't speak to anymore.

If you want to try writing a thank-you on your own, consider these points:

Be specific.

A good thank-you note references the actual thing you were given or act someone performed for you: "the recommendation you provided," "the party you threw," "the bail money you posted."

Embrace hyperbole.

You should exaggerate a little, but not so much that the recipient will think you insincere. It's OK to write, "Thank you for the best dinner I've had this year." But saying, "I had dinner at Per Se three times last week and not once did it compare to your meatloaf" is probably going overboard.

Get in, get out.

No one expects you to write a small novel to express your appreciation, so get your point across in three to six sentences. This makes you more mysterious. Plus, most people want you to hurry up so they can get back to watching TV.

APOLOGIES

You are not fabulous if you cannot admit you behaved badly. The best way to apologize to someone you've insulted or wronged is to invite her to speak with you privately. Look her in the eyes and say, "I'm sorry for ___. You didn't deserve that, and I won't let it happen again." If you're filling in the blank with things like "raising my voice at you," "saying your haircut looked like a mullet," or "telling the neighborhood you stole that ambrosia recipe from me," a verbal apology will suffice.

If you're filling in the blank with things like, "distributing the Christmas party picture where your boob is popping out," or "telling that cute guy you have herpes," you should follow up your conversation with a small bouquet of flowers.

THE THEATER

Attending live theater is one of the few activities that separate human beings from the other primates. And unfortunately, most people haven't a clue how to behave when seeing a show. My Seven Cardinal Rules for Broadway, Off-Broadway, the opera, the ballet, and touring groups:

1. Wear something nice. Your fellow theatergoers are paying for the entire experience, which includes being surrounded by fabulous people.
2. When entering a row in which people are already sitting, shimmy in facing the stage. It's better to put your buttocks in someone's face than your reproductive organs.
3. Don't be a hair-hopper. The legitimate theater is no place for a leftover Whitesnake groupie. The person behind you purchased a view also.
4. Keep your head fairly still. I had to get snippy with a woman in front of me recently because her head was bopping like a metronome, and I hate having to get snippy.
5. Turn your cell phone OFF, not on vibrate. Vibrate makes noise, ya dope.
6. Unwrap your candy before the show. And don't crunch it.
7. Don't watch the entire show, then leave right before or *during* curtain call just so you can be the first one to catch a cab. How incredibly rude to deprive the cast of their applause! The next time I see you do this I might "accidentally" stick my foot in the aisle and trip you.

OPENING DOORS FOR WOMEN

Once upon a time, the rules of etiquette were crystal clear about opening doors: Men held them and women walked through them. End of story. But now that women vote, hold powerful positions in business and politics, and are responsible for their own orgasms, the average man has no idea whether to hold open a door or to walk right through it.

In business situations, whoever arrives at a door first should open it and hold it open for the other members of the group. There's no need to make a big ole fuss about it.

In social situations, it's still polite for a man to hold a door for a woman. It's also polite for a man to hold the door for another man. Or a woman can hold the door for another woman. You see, the world is just a nicer place when we all hold doors for each other.

Revolving doors make things just slightly more complicated. In business, whoever arrives at a revolving door first should enter first. In a social situation, if a revolving door is in the process of revolving, the woman should step in first and the man can follow in the next compartment. If the door is stationary, the man can enter first to get the thing moving. Just use common sense. Yes, most women have the strength to push a revolving door on their own, but a guy should step up to the plate, so to speak, if his date is wearing stilettos, holding a cashmere wrap around her shoulders, and carrying a clutch because—because, duh, you can't get good traction in stilettos.

THE TAXI SCOOCH

A man and a woman on a date in New York City hail a taxi. When the taxi pulls over, the man opens the door. What should he say next to his date?

a) *"After you."*
b) *Nothing—he should get in first.*
c) *"Would you like me to scooch?"*
d) *"I'll get in on the other side."*

The answer is C or D, depending on the traffic. If there's no traffic, the man should close the door for the woman and tell her that he'll enter the taxi on the other side. If by doing so he'd risk a 45-mile-an-hour grille to the kneecaps, he should give the woman the option of getting in second, so she doesn't have to scooch across the backseat. Scooching sucks and nobody likes doing it.

SMOKING

Smoking is not fabulous—unless it is 1998 and you are slightly f#&*ed-up at a party in Paris, surrounded by fashion designers, artists, editors, models, and actors who are all smoking. Then it is fabulous and you are fabulous and life is fabulous. God, I miss my 20s.

Never smoke in someone's else's house. Never smoke in a nonsmoking section. Never smoke indoors when a child is in the same room. Never smoke around sick people. Go outside and be by yourself or with the other smokers. Haven't you heard? That stuff will kill you.

BEING A GOOD GUEST

FASHIONABLE LATENESS

The term "fashionably late" applies only to cocktail parties.

There is no such thing as being "fashionably late" when hot food will be served, such as a friend's dinner party, a luncheon, a wedding, or dinner at a restaurant. If you will be more than 15 minutes late, do everything in your power to let your companions know of your situation via phone call or text message at the very least. When you arrive, apologize but not profusely. Nothing is lamer than listening to someone drone on about how their cat choked on a furball and their landlord turned off the hot water and their five-inch heel got stuck in a subway grate. Just move on, Sally.

Cocktail parties are another story. If I invite 50 friends over for drinks and hors d'oeuvres at 9:00 p.m., everyone knows that the party will just be getting started at 10:00 p.m. In fact, my friends have been trained to expect that if they arrive on time, I will put them to work making canapés or polishing the glassware. Actually, I find that early arrivals don't mind helping out a little bit, as it takes a little edge off the awkwardness of having been the first to arrive. And we get to spend some quality time together.

For cocktail parties, fashionable lateness will vary by city. In New York, an hour or two is no big whoop. In Cincinnati, a half hour to an hour is your window. In Barcelona, expect people about four hours late, if they show up at all.

LATENESS IN GENERAL

Chronic tardiness severely affects your fabulousness quotient because being fabulous means that you respect and encourage other people's fabulousness. When you continually keep other people waiting, you're basically implying that their time is less important than yours. That's not fabulous. That's moronic.

TRUE OR FALSE:

You should never arrive at a party empty-handed.

FALSE. A good host doesn't expect you to bring anything because everything has been thought of in advance. (See "How to Entertain" on page 162.) But bringing a small token of your appreciation for being invited is certainly not uncouth. However, do not bring:

FLOWERS. While any civilized person enjoys receiving flowers, she does not want to be confronted with them while she's entertaining. The hostess of a party has a lot on her mind—food, beverages, music, temperature, mingling—and being forced to find a vase and trim stems and discard the wrapping can throw her off her game. Plus, they might interfere with her decorating scheme. Instead, have your flowers delivered the next day accompanied by a small thank-you note.

WINE YOU EXPECT TO BE SERVED. Wine is a very appropriate gift, as long as your host is not underage or an alcoholic or an underage alcoholic. But never expect the wine you bring to a party to be served at that party. A conscientious host has already chosen wines for the evening based on what will pair well with the hors d'oeuvres. Or perhaps the party is New Zealand–themed and your Chianti doesn't exactly fit in. NEVER leave with the wine you brought because the bottle wasn't opened.

FOOD THAT HAS NOT BEEN REQUESTED. If I want seven-layer taco dip served at my party, I'll ask you to bring it or I'll make it myself, thank you. Can I make myself any clearer, Aunt Debbie?

Oh, Serena, you brought dessert. You shouldn't have. No, really, you shouldn't have. Now you've ruined my entire party. Everyone, Serena ruined the party. Booo, Serena.

If you would like to bring something, I've got a few suggestions: a small box of quality chocolates, a good book, pretty cocktail napkins, a jar of herbs de Provence, coasters. (I even received a bag of tiny umbrellas once. I never used them, but I thought they were a cute gift at the time.) Don't forget to attach a little card with your name on it, something your host will appreciate the next morning.

The best way to score an invite to the next chic party is a thank you delivered via e-mail or a phone call within 48 hours or flowers or another small gift within seven days.

The best ways to get yourself removed from future party invite lists:

- *Bringing an uninvited guest.*
- *Getting sloppy drunk (and by sloppy, I don't mean slurring words because that's funny! I mean breaking stuff and/or puking somewhere other than in the toilet).*
- *Making sexist, racist, homophobic, or religiously insensitive comments. Those just make you a jerk.*

HOW TO HANDLE BREAKAGE

Every once in a while a guest will accidentally break something at a party. A good host knowingly accepts this risk and never makes a big deal about a spilled drink or a chipped serving dish. Should someone break a glass in your kitchen, just clean it up quietly, assure your guest that she committed no crime, and get her a new one. If someone accidentally breaks your 17th-century Persian statuette that was perched on an end table, it's your fault for not moving it to a more secure location in the first place.

You should never ask a guest to pay for something he broke—unless that guest was incredibly careless and out of control. However, if you served that guest too much alcohol, you are partially responsible for his actions. In any case, a conversation about compensation should wait until the next day.

Congratulations!

You now know how to behave fabulously and are only four chapters away from being Freakin' Fabulous!

HOW TO EAT

Fabulous people dine out a lot. I could tell you they do this because they possess a natural curiosity regarding exotic cuisines, because they enjoy taking in the smart décor of certain restaurants, and because they like to be surrounded by other fabulous people. This would all be true. But most of the time they eat out because they're too damn tired (or lazy) to cook.

However—and this is a big however—fabulous people can absolutely whip up a delicious meal without fear when they need to or want to. In fact, all fabulous people know four recipes by heart, and I must insist that you commit them to memory as well. Yes, memory. As in, *memorize* them. You may consult a cookbook for other recipes but absolutely not for these.

THE FREAKIN' FABULOUS FOUR:

HOLLANDAISE

ROASTED CHICKEN

A FRENCH OMELET

A NICE VINAIGRETTE

Fab Four Recipes

HOLLANDAISE

Most people don't know this, but "hollandaise" is French for "there's a pain in my chest radiating down my left arm." So I wouldn't recommend eating more than a few spoonfuls at any given time. It's probably also best if you eat only steamed carrots for the following week.

But think of how impressed your friends will be when they've invited you to stay over for the weekend and you just "whip up a batch of hollandaise to go with that gorgeous asparagus you bought at the farmer's market." (Yes, in my world, people speak like this.)

YOU NEED:

A DOUBLE BOILER

2 EGG YOLKS

2 TEASPOONS FRESH LEMON JUICE

2 TEASPOONS WATER

2 STICKS BUTTER, MELTED AND KEPT WARM

SALT AND WHITE PEPPER

In a double boiler, whisk together the egg yolks, lemon juice, and water.

Cook until the mixture thickens (to a runny whipped-cream texture).

Add the butter slowly—whisking constantly—until incorporated.

Remove from the heat. Add salt and pepper to taste. (If you use black pepper instead of white pepper, it's not the end of the world, but you will have little black dots in your hollandaise, which to some is a no-no.)

If you want, throw in some finely chopped shallots and some fresh tarragon with the egg yolks, lemon juice, and water. It's practically a béarnaise—my favorite sauce on the planet. Serve it with a grilled, medium-rare steak and I'll be your best friend. (This is why my triglycerides are through the roof.)

YIELD: 1 CUP (2 TO 4 SERVINGS)

Hollandaise
sauce

ROASTED CHICKEN

I've made this dish about 500 times and not once has it failed me. If it fails you, you have done something wrong. It'll be a cold day in hell before I let you blame me.

YOU NEED:

1 ROASTING CHICKEN (4 TO 5 POUNDS)

A BUNCH OF FRESH HERBS (SAGE, THYME, ROSEMARY, OR A COMBINATION THEREOF)

1 LEMON

KITCHEN STRING

SOME BUTTER, SOFTENED

SALT AND PEPPER

A ROASTING PAN

Preheat the oven to 425°F.

Rinse the chicken inside and out, discarding anything that has been wrapped in paper and stuffed back into the cavity. Towel-dry the chicken to ensure that the skin crisps nicely.

Stuff the herbs into the chicken cavity. Poke a bunch of holes into the lemon with a knife or fork, and stuff the lemon inside as well.

Truss the chicken and then rub the chicken skin with butter. Sprinkle with salt and pepper. Place in a roasting pan and put in the oven.

Roast for 20 minutes. (This sears the skin and seals in the juices.) Reduce heat to 350°F and cook for 15 minutes per pound. (A 4-pound chicken cooks for an additional one hour, a 5-pound chicken for an additional hour and 15 minutes. Get it?)

Remove from the oven and let sit for 15 minutes.

Carve.

YIELD: 4 SERVINGS

CHICKEN*

french
omelet

A FRENCH OMELET

French omelets are fluffier and runnier than their American counterparts. They also contain a *merde*-load of butter. Yum! The keys to making a good one: Keep the eggs moving until they set, and tilt your pan to regulate the heat. Once you've got the basic technique down, you can add any number of fillings. Serve with some mixed, lightly dressed greens and a glass of Sancerre for an early dinner, and I guarantee you will get laid. You also might get salmonella, but the chances of getting laid are much higher.

YOU NEED:

3 LARGE (OR 2 JUMBO) EGGS

PINCHES OF SALT AND PEPPER

FRESH CHOPPED HERBS *(in an ideal world, chives, parsley, tarragon, and chervil)*

1 TABLESPOON BUTTER

SMALL, PREFERABLY NONSTICK, OMELET PAN

A STIFF SPATULA

Whisk together the eggs, salt, pepper, and a small handful of whatever fresh herbs you've got on hand, keeping in mind that some are more powerful than others.

In your omelet pan, over high heat, melt the butter.

When the butter stops foaming, pour in the eggs. (If the butter burns, discard and start over.)

Keep the eggs moving by stirring constantly with your spatula.

When the eggs look like they're about to set, tilt the omelet pan away from you at a 45-degree angle so that most of the egg mixture falls to the other side of the pan.

Let cook about 30 seconds longer.

Fold the thinner side down onto the thicker side.

Roll the omelet onto a plate so that any seam is invisible.

YIELD: 1 SERVING

Vinaigrette
he Swedish coun-
ade even more en-
mirrors that heighten
are designed by Monica
for Boda and are hand-pain
jersey dress
nnamodeller, $55). The
the field of ripening grain wears
by Bertil Wahl (Bloom-

A NICE VINAIGRETTE

I used to be in awe of anyone who could throw together a vinaigrette without looking at a recipe. That is, until I actually took 5 minutes to look at a recipe and realized it was hardly rocket science. Most people will tell you that the standard ratio for a vinaigrette is one part vinegar to three parts oil. I prefer to start with one part vinegar to four parts oil because it's easier to add more vinegar to acidify your dressing after tasting it than it is to dilute one with more oil.

Before you foodies get on my case, I know this isn't the most thrilling vinaigrette in the world. I highly encourage any reader to add shallots, substitute champagne vinegar or raspberry vinegar, use stone-ground mustard, add a touch of honey, whatever. But first, you must get this one correct!

YOU NEED:

4 TABLESPOONS EXTRA-VIRGIN OLIVE OIL

1 TABLESPOON BALSAMIC VINEGAR

1 TABLESPOON DIJON MUSTARD

1 CLOVE GARLIC, MINCED

PINCHES OF SALT AND PEPPER

Combine everything in a bowl. Whisk it together. Makes just enough dressing for one of those prewashed bags of mixed lettuce. Save any extra in the fridge for about a week in an airtight container.

YIELD: 1 CUP (2 TO 4 SERVINGS)

TEN OTHER FREAKIN' THINGS YOU NEED TO KNOW

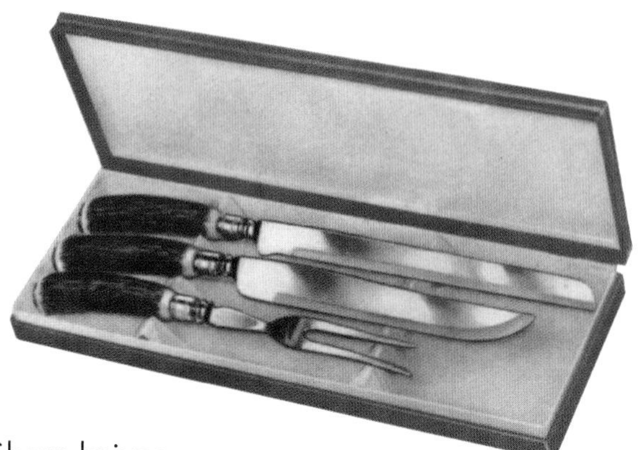

1 HOW TO USE A KNIFE

I highly recommend taking a knife-skills class when available. They're often offered as a single session in adult education programs and will save you a ton of time—and perhaps a liter of blood—while you're prepping your next meal.

Most importantly, your knife must be sharp. Sharp knives actually result in fewer cut fingers because you won't have to force the knife as much and it's less likely to skid or slide away from where you're intending it to go. If you don't have a knife-sharpening service near you, inquire at a local hardware store. And if that's not an option, most high-end kitchen-supply companies sell pretty good knife sharpeners.

When cutting, make sure your surface is solid and sturdy. There will be nicks and cuts on the surface beneath your food by the time you're through, which is why a wood or plastic cutting board is best. If the board is slipping a little, a damp hand towel placed between the board and the counter should keep things steady.

When cutting food, leave the tip of the knife on the cutting board and use your wrist to move only the handle up and down. This method is quicker and makes it less likely that your fingers will get in between the knife and the cutting board.

Keep your fingers curled and your thumb tucked behind the knife when guiding food. That will keep them away from the blade.

Choose consistency over speed . . . food cooks better if all the pieces are the same size.

HOW TO CHOP AN ONION

Cut off the stem end of the onion. Remove the "paper" and tough outer layer.

Place the onion on its now-flat surface and cut in half through the root. Take one half of the onion and lay it flat on your cutting board.

Make several horizontal cuts into the onion toward the root but not through it. Make several vertical cuts, once again being careful not to cut through the root.

Holding the onion steady—fingers curled away from the blade—cut down toward the cutting board.

Stop crying, ya big baby.

Hot Tip

If chopping onions makes you cry, hold a few unlit matches in your mouth. The sulfur is supposed to absorb some of the onion fumes. You can also hold a slice of white bread in your mouth. Either way, you'll look like an idiot. Also, try throwing the onion in the freezer for a bit before you chop it. The colder the onion, the less fumes. Personally, I don't mind a good cry. In fact, if I cry while chopping onions, I'll run to the bathroom mirror and recite one of my favorite lines from *Poltergeist:* "Don't you touch my babies!!!" It's the part where the kids are being sucked into the bedroom closet for the second time and JoBeth Williams is at HER WIT'S END! It's very dramatic. (Hi, JoBeth, if you're reading this!!!)

3 HOW TO CHOP GARLIC

Remove a garlic clove from the head. Leave the peel on.

Place the clove on a cutting board. Cover it with the flat side of a thick, stiff knife and give it a good smack. (It's by far the fastest way to remove the skin but also the most dangerous if you have an IQ under 50. Point the blade away from you and use the heel of your hand.)

Discard the peel. Give the garlic one more squish and look, it's half chopped.

Rock the blade of your knife back and forth over it a few more times and you're good to go.

Hot Tip

After chopping or handling garlic, squeeze a little lemon juice on your fingers to neutralize the smell and wash them off in cold water (hot water makes the smell set). This also works on cutting boards. Make sure to do this before shaking hands with anyone or before you switch to another recipe . . . you don't want your dessert to smell like garlic.

You can also run your hands on something stainless steel, like a utensil, a pot or pan, or even your sink. My friend Gaby gave me a bar of stainless-steel "soap" for Christmas last year. Merry freakin' Christmas.

HOW TO POACH A CHICKEN BREAST

This is all I eat for two weeks before any trip to Miami. Also good to know for chicken salad and other cold dishes.

Hot Tip

If you accidentally add too much salt to a recipe, cut up a potato into large chunks and throw it in for a while. It will absorb some of the salt and you can remove it later. But let's face it, you're probably screwed.

Put boneless, skinless chicken breasts into a sauté pan. Add enough chicken stock to fully cover the chicken. (You might have to weigh down the chicken breasts with a small plate.)

Over medium heat, bring to a light simmer—not a rolling boil.

Turn off the heat. Cover and let the chicken return to room temperature.

Note: You can add all sorts of herbs, onions, and vegetables to the stock if you want. I don't think all that hoo-ha is necessary as long as you're using a flavorful stock.

5 HOW TO HARD-BOIL AN EGG

Place eggs in a saucepan in a single layer. Cover with cool water so that there's at least an inch of water on top. (Fresher eggs will sink, older eggs will float, but either will do as long as they're not rancid.)

Bring the water to a boil on high heat. Reduce the heat, bringing the water to a simmer. Simmer for 1 minute.

Turn off the stove. Cover the pot and let the water cool to room temperature.

Perfect every time!

HOW TO SEPARATE AN EGG

Bang the egg lightly on a flat surface. Press your thumbs into the indentation. Holding the egg above a bowl, separate the two halves of the shell so they look like two little cups.

Gently move the yolk back and forth between the two little cups. The whites will fall out into the bowl below.

Or you could crack an egg into your hand. Let the whites fall through your fingers.

HOW TO POACH AN EGG

Fill a large frying pan or skillet with 2 to 3 inches of water, lightly salted, and bring to a boil. Some people add a drop of vinegar to the water to keep the whites together. Personally, I don't think it's necessary.

Crack an egg into a shallow dish, using the freshest eggs possible.

Reduce the water to barely a simmer. Slide the egg into the water. Set a timer for 3½ minutes.

When the white becomes translucent, gently flip the egg.

Remove the egg with a slotted spoon. Towel-dry with a paper towel.

Transfer to toast or an English muffin.

A friend of mine swears by these cute silicone cups that keep your eggs from creating a sloppy mess during the poaching process, but I don't know. I guess I'm just old-fashioned because I like watching the egg spread out in the water like a ghost!

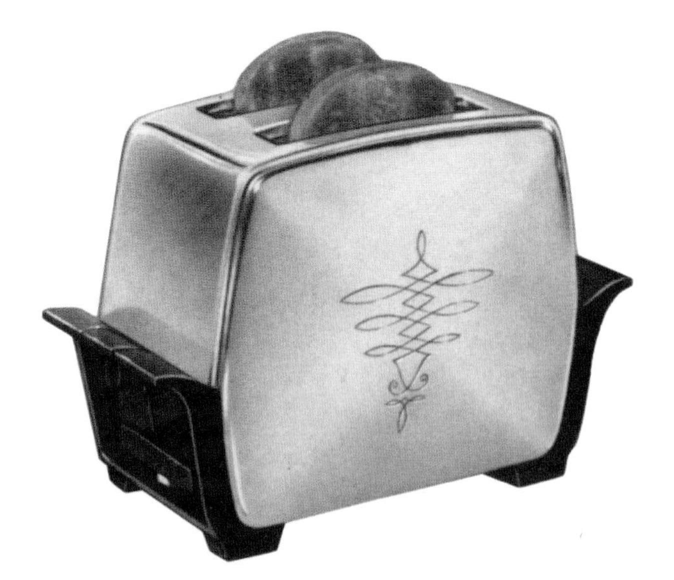

ached
Eggs

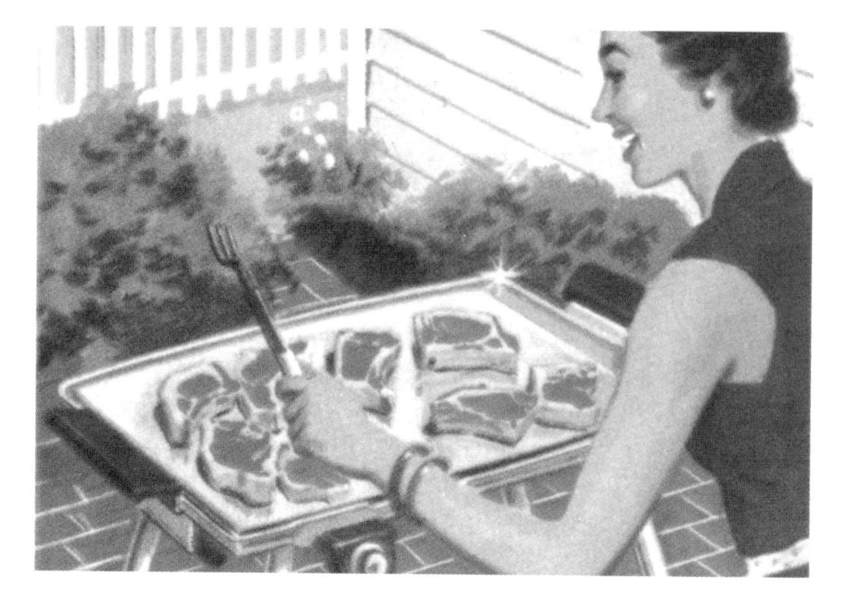

HOW TO TELL WHEN A STEAK IS DONE

The more you cook steak, the better you'll get at touching it to tell its doneness. You want to avoid cutting into the steak if you can; doing so will release some of its juices.

VERY RARE STEAK *(still bloody in the center and barely warm): feels very soft to the touch and will bounce back when poked*

RARE STEAK *(red in the center and just a little warm): feels soft to the touch*

MEDIUM-RARE STEAK *(pinkish red in the center): yields slightly to the touch*

MEDIUM STEAK *(pink in the center): yields only slightly to the touch, beginning to firm up*

MEDIUM-WELL STEAK *(grayish pink in the center): firm to the touch*

WELL-DONE STEAK *(gray throughout): hard to the touch*

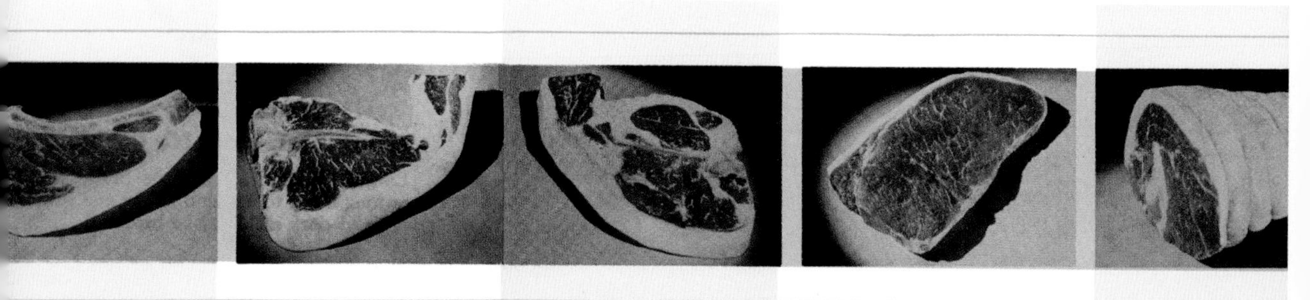

HOW TO MAKE MAYONNAISE

I make my mayonnaise in a mini food processor, but you can also use a bowl and a whisk.

YOU NEED:

2 EGG YOLKS

1 TABLESPOON DIJON MUSTARD

1 CUP VEGETABLE OIL
(olive oil works but will produce a strong olive oil flavor)

1 TABLESPOON LEMON JUICE

SALT AND FRESHLY GROUND PEPPER

Combine the egg yolks and mustard and pulse until blended.

Add the oil in a VERY slow stream until it's all incorporated. Don't rush!

When the mixture is very creamy, add the lemon juice.

Season with salt and pepper to taste.

YIELD: 1 CUP

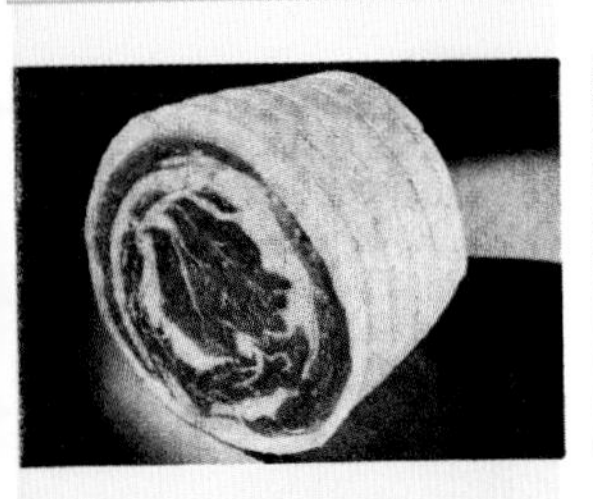

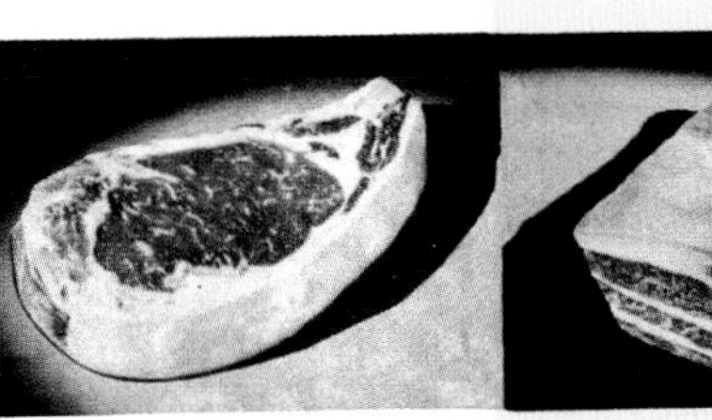

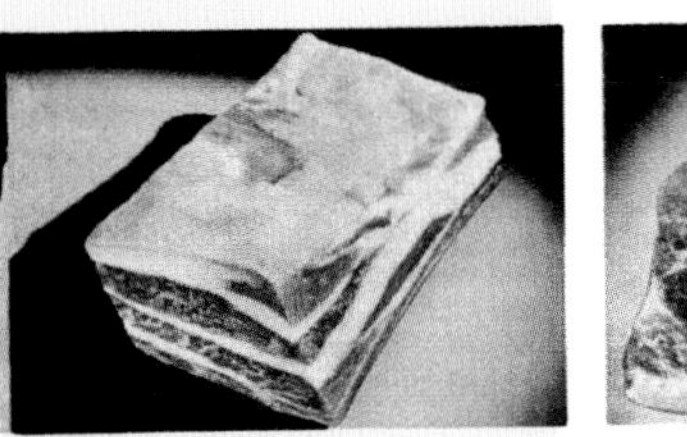

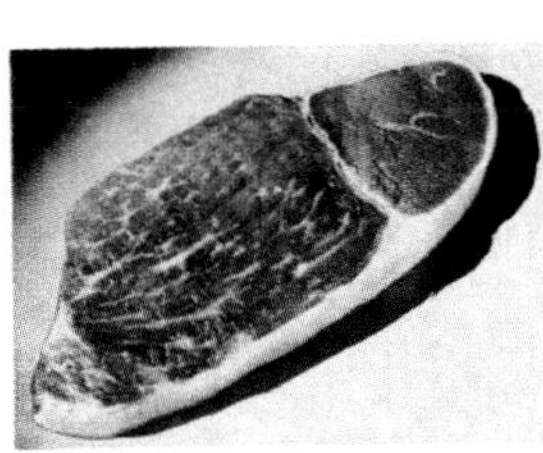

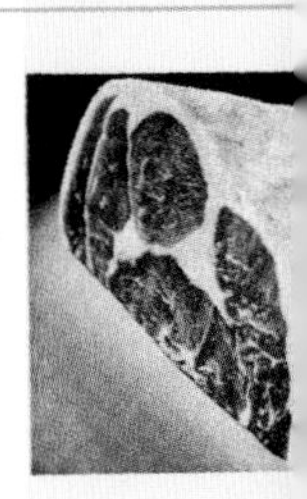

HOW TO MAKE WHIPPED CREAM

About 10 minutes before you're ready to start whipping, throw the container of whipping cream into the freezer, along with a stainless-steel bowl and a balloon whisk (or the whipping attachment for your beater).

When everything's chilled, add 2 tablespoons of confectioner's sugar and a dash of vanilla extract (the good stuff, not imitation) for every cup of whipping cream.

If you're using a beater, whisk on high speed for about 1 minute; if by hand, about 2 minutes. (Whisk longer if you're whipping more than 1 cup of cream.)

Stop when the cream forms soft peaks. (Soft peaks look like waves lapping against the shore. Stiff peaks, on the other hand, which are usually what you want when making meringues, will stand straight up in the air, like spiky mountains.)

FIVE RECIPES YOU CAN'T SCREW UP

Well, maybe you could. But try not to.

Steak Au Poivre

This delicious dish, "steak with pepper" in French, always seems to impress my carnivorous dinner guests. You can serve it with a lightly dressed green salad or some steamed asparagus and perhaps a few roasted potatoes.

It's the perfect "seal the deal" meal. That is, if you've gone on a few dates with a guy and you want him to fall in love with you, cook him this steak. Men are suckers for beef.

YOU NEED:

2 TABLESPOONS WHOLE BLACK PEPPERCORNS

ONE 16-OUNCE STRIP STEAK CUT IN TWO PIECES *(You could also use two 8-ounce sirloins. Either way, the steaks should be at least 1 inch thick. Trim any excess fat.)*

SALT

1 TABLESPOON BUTTER

1 TEASPOON OLIVE OIL

2 SHALLOTS, MINCED

¼ CUP COGNAC *(Bourbon is also nice or a Madeira)*

½ CUP HEAVY CREAM

YIELD: 2 SERVINGS

The peppercorns in steak au poivre should be very coarsely crushed. You can do this with a mortar and pestle or by placing them on a hard surface and pressing down on them with a heavy skillet.

Salt the steaks. Then press the steaks—both sides—into the cracked peppercorns.

In a heavy skillet over medium heat, melt the butter and olive oil. When the skillet gets very hot, add the steaks, and cook for about 2 minutes. (You want a nice brown color on the meat.) Turn the steaks over and cook for another 2 minutes. At this point, your steaks will be rare to medium-rare. Don't overcook them. It's always easier to throw a steak back in a pan for a few minutes than to convert shoe leather back into something edible.

Once the steaks reach the desired doneness, remove them and place on a plate, lightly covered with aluminum foil. This will keep them warm, but the steaks will also continue cooking a little—all the reason not to overcook them in the first place.

To the pan, add the minced shallots and stir to scrape any delicious bits that have stuck to the bottom.

Now, here comes the fire!

Remove the pan from the stove and add the Cognac. You have two choices: 1. You can ignite the Cognac with a long matchstick; or 2. Return the pan to the stove, keeping your face away from it, and tilt it so that the flame from the stove ignites the Cognac vapors.

When the flames die, add the cream. Bring the mixture to a boil and stir for another 5 minutes or so, until the sauce thickens. Add the steaks back to the pan, coat with sauce, and serve.

YIELD: 2 SERVINGS

Sole Picatta

This dish is very light, so it works well in warmer weather when your guests might not want a heavy steak. It's also quite elegant for an intimate dinner—quite worthy of your best china. Serve with some steamed haricot verts and some boiled new potatoes.

YOU NEED:

- 2 TABLESPOONS OLIVE OIL
- 4 DOVER SOLE FILLETS
- SALT AND PEPPER
- ALL-PURPOSE FLOUR
- ½ CUP DRY WHITE WINE
- 2 TABLESPOONS BUTTER
- 1 TABLESPOON DIJON MUSTARD
- 1 TABLESPOON DRAINED CAPERS
- 1 TABLESPOON CHOPPED FRESH PARSLEY

Heat the oil in a large, nonstick skillet over medium-high heat.

Sprinkle the sole with salt and pepper, and dust both sides with flour. Add the fish to the skillet and cook until lightly browned, about 2 minutes per side. Transfer the fish to a plate.

Add the wine and butter to the same skillet. Bring the mixture to a boil, stirring up any browned bits. Add the mustard, capers, and parsley. Simmer until the sauce is slightly thickened, about 3 minutes. Season with salt and pepper and serve.

YIELD: 4 SERVINGS

Osso Bucco

When I invite people to my house in Connecticut in the winter, I love to make dishes that can simmer on top of the stove for hours, filling the air with savory goodness. The ingredient list is fairly long for this, but once you've got it all in the pot, you don't have to worry too much about it. Serve this with some crusty bread and a hearty red wine. Perfect for a cold winter's night.

YOU NEED:

ABOUT 3 POUNDS OF VEAL SHANK *(ask your butcher to cut it into pieces that are about 2 inches thick)*

SALT AND PEPPER

ALL-PURPOSE FLOUR

2 TABLESPOONS OLIVE OIL

2 MEDIUM ONIONS, CHOPPED

2 CARROTS, DICED

2 CELERY STALKS, DICED

6 LARGE CLOVES GARLIC, CHOPPED

ONE 28-OUNCE CAN PEELED ITALIAN PLUM TOMATOES, CRUSHED

2 CUPS LOW-SALT BEEF STOCK

1 CUP DRY WHITE WINE

2 BAY LEAVES

½ TEASPOON GRATED LEMON PEEL

YIELD: 2 TO 4 SERVINGS

Lightly salt and pepper the veal shanks and dredge in flour. Shake off any excess.

Over medium-high flame, heat the oil in a Dutch oven. Add the shanks to the pot and cook until brown, turning occasionally. Don't overload the pot with the shanks. If you have to cook them in two batches, do so. Each batch will take 12 to 15 minutes. Transfer the shanks to a platter when brown.

Reduce the heat slightly. Add the onions, carrots, and celery to the pot, and sauté until tender, about 3 minutes. Add the garlic and sauté another minute. Return the shanks and any liquid they've released back to the pot. Add the tomatoes, stock, wine, bay leaves, and lemon peel to the pot.

Let that mixture come to a boil, then reduce the heat to a very low setting. Cover partially and simmer for at least 2 hours. (I've even made it 5 hours in advance of dinner. If too much of the sauce evaporates, you can add a little more wine or some more stock.) The meat should be very tender and falling off the bones.

Remove the bay leaves and serve.

The Best Turkey Meatballs Ever (and a nice sauce)

I'm half Italian, so I was 18 years old and in college before I knew that you could buy pasta sauce in a *jar* at the supermarket. (I'm not even kidding.) My mother and my nanna would have fed the family rusted fishing hooks covered in motor oil before even considering buying a premade sauce.

So, I always make my own tomato-based sauces, and I experiment a lot. Sometimes the results are good and sometimes they're amazing. Below is a recipe for an impromptu sauce with turkey meatballs that I made one night.

By the way, I'd tell you the family recipe for sauce, but I'm afraid my family would put a hit out on me. (Plus, I think we all hold dreams of canning the stuff and selling it in supermarkets worldwide.)

FOR THE MEATBALLS:

1 PACKAGE GROUND TURKEY
(about 1¼ pounds)

2 EGGS

ABOUT ¾ CUP BREAD CRUMBS

ABOUT 1 TABLESPOON OREGANO

ABOUT 1 TABLESPOON ROSEMARY, CRUSHED

6 TO 8 BIG DASHES OF HOT SAUCE

½ LARGE ONION, DICED
(you'll use the other half in the sauce)

3 LARGE CLOVES GARLIC, MINCED

SALT AND PEPPER

Mix all the ingredients up. The mixture is pretty mushy, unlike beef meatballs.

Form into 24 meatballs and place on a sheet pan coated with nonstick spray. Bake at 400°F for about 12 minutes. Reduce the heat to 350°F for another 15 minutes or so.

FOR THE SAUCE:

SOME OLIVE OIL

3 LARGE CLOVES GARLIC, MINCED

½ LARGE ONION, DICED

ONE 28-OUNCE CAN MUIR GLEN ORGANIC CHUNKY TOMATO SAUCE
(It's unflavored but very delicious.)

SOME OREGANO

SOME ROSEMARY

ABOUT ½ CUP ROMANO CHEESE

ABOUT 8 FRESH BASIL LEAVES

A DASH OF SWEET VERMOUTH

Heat the oil in a large skillet over medium heat. Sauté the garlic and onions until translucent. Add the tomato sauce and everything else. Let it simmer until the meatballs are done. Add the meatballs and let it simmer some more. Serve with some pasta and more Romano cheese. You are going to FREAK OUT, THESE ARE SO GOOD!

YIELD: 4 TO 6 SERVINGS

CREAM PUFFS!

ARE YOU **READY?** Because I'm about to change your life. Once you realize how easy it is to make cream puff shells, they're going to start appearing at all your parties—during all courses! Take it from me, your friends will think you're a genius. I won't tell them the truth. Oooh, snap!

YOU NEED:

1 CUP WATER
1 STICK BUTTER
1 CUP FLOUR
4 EGGS

(continued)

Cream
Puffs

Cream Puffs! (continued)

In a medium saucepan, boil the water and the butter. Bring to a simmer and stir in the flour—not all at once but about ¼ cup at a time. The mixture will become a big ball.

Let that blob cool to room temperature.

Preheat your oven to 400°F.

Transfer the blob to a large mixing bowl. Using a slow setting on your electric beater (or your hands), add the eggs one at a time. Don't add the next egg until the previous one has been incorporated. Beat until smooth and velvety.

Lightly coat a cookie sheet with nonstick spray (or use a Silpat liner).

Drop the batter in 8 large spoonfuls on the cookie sheet and bake for 45 minutes.

Note: Using the same amount of batter, I will often make 12 smaller puffs and cook them for about 35 minutes. In either case, keep an eye on them. They should be a medium-golden brown and DRY on the outside, or else they'll collapse when you take them out of the oven to cool.

YIELD: 8 TO 12 SERVINGS

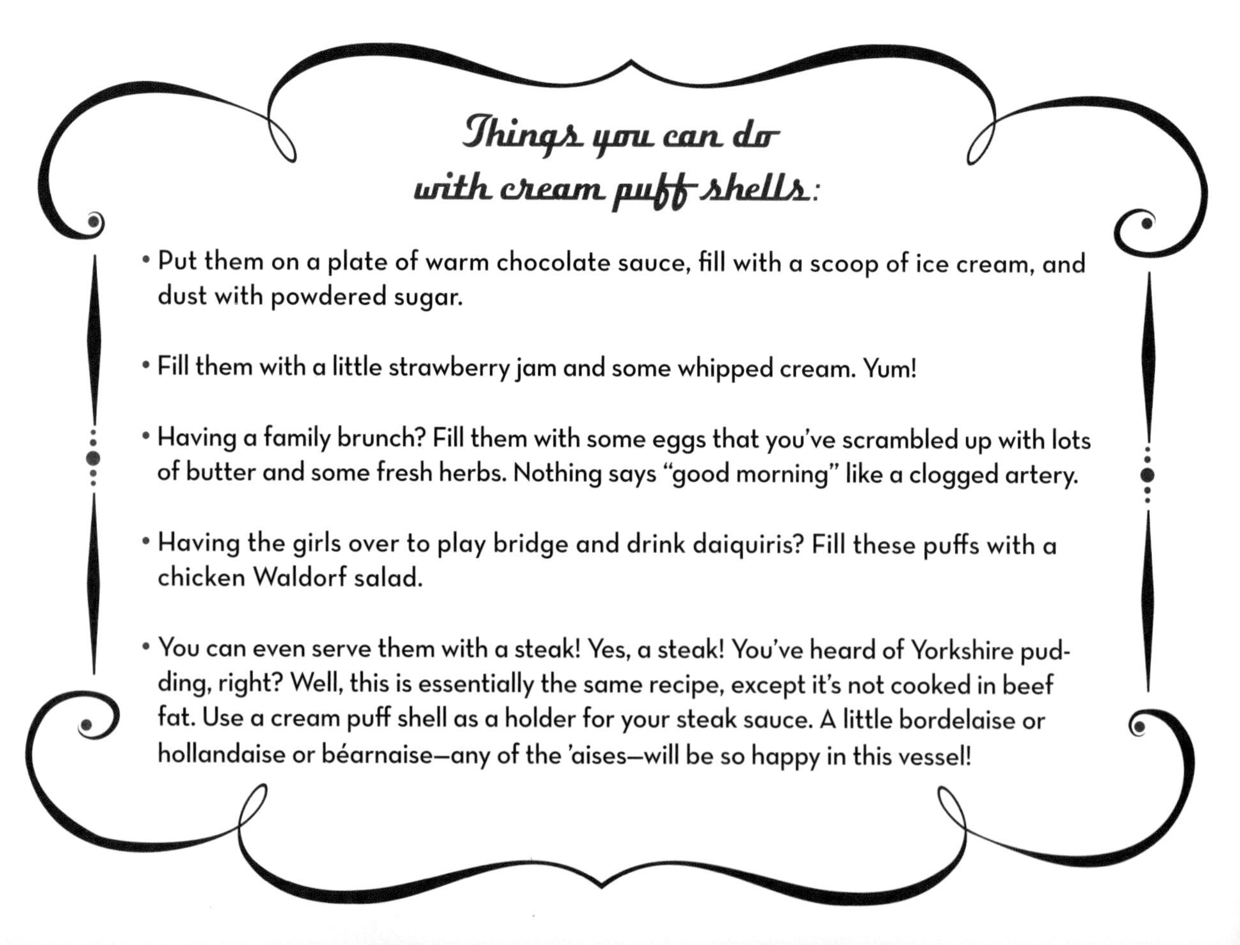

Things you can do with cream puff shells:

- Put them on a plate of warm chocolate sauce, fill with a scoop of ice cream, and dust with powdered sugar.
- Fill them with a little strawberry jam and some whipped cream. Yum!
- Having a family brunch? Fill them with some eggs that you've scrambled up with lots of butter and some fresh herbs. Nothing says "good morning" like a clogged artery.
- Having the girls over to play bridge and drink daiquiris? Fill these puffs with a chicken Waldorf salad.
- You can even serve them with a steak! Yes, a steak! You've heard of Yorkshire pudding, right? Well, this is essentially the same recipe, except it's not cooked in beef fat. Use a cream puff shell as a holder for your steak sauce. A little bordelaise or hollandaise or béarnaise—any of the 'aises—will be so happy in this vessel!

Freakin' Fab

Congratulations!

FF

You now know how to eat fabulously and are only three chapters away from being Freakin' Fabulous!

HOW TO DRINK

"Gin has made me do
a lot of stupid
things, but
I forgive it."
— Clinton Kelly

Fabulous people have signature "drinks." For example, my drink has always been the gin and tonic. Having a "drink" has made it easier on my friends, who now know to have gin and tonic on hand if they ask me to visit. (I drink wine with dinner, of course. I'm not a savage.)

Recently, I've added another drink to my repertoire, the Manhattan. This has become my fall/winter drink. So, I'll take a gin and tonic from Memorial Day to Labor Day and a Manhattan from Labor Day to Memorial Day, weather permitting. That is, if I'm in Palm Springs in March and there's not a cloud in the sky and the thermometer reads 85 degrees, I'll have the gin and tonic. To be fabulous, you must go with the flow.

The tricky thing about drinking is that too much of it can make you act like a schmuck. Schmucks are not even close to fabulous. If you don't drink, please don't feel less fabulous. I have great respect for people who have decided not to drink, for whatever reason, although I doubt I'll ever be one of them.

On the following pages, you'll find recipes for the most fabulous drinks. You will not find appletinis or Alabama slammers or screaming orgasms mentioned anywhere. That's because I don't care for them. Tough noogies.

GIN

Most people assume gin was invented by the British, but they would be wrong. It was the glorious Dutch who get the credit for introducing the most fabulous of liquors to the world. In the early 17th century, gin was sold as medicine—that means it's good for you! Gin's distinct flavor comes from the juniper berry, which contains many antioxidants—that means it's doubly good for you!

As far as I'm concerned, there are only four gin drinks that matter, and the one that matters the most is the GIN AND TONIC. (It never ceases to amaze me that when somebody says, "GIN AND TONIC," the skies open up, sunshine beats down on my face, and angels sing to me. It's freaky!) Here's how you make the perfect . . . **GIN AND TONIC.**

Fill a glass with ice made from pure spring water.

Add some of your favorite gin.

Add twice as much tonic water as you did gin. (You must get this part right: It's two parts tonic to one part gin.)

Squeeze a lime wedge into the glass.

Stir gently. Thank the angels for stopping by.

THE OTHER THREE GIN DRINKS THAT MATTER:

THE MARTINI
THE GIBSON
THE GIMLET

THE MARTINI

Before I give you the perfect recipe, there are three things you must know about The Martini.

1. A true one is made with gin. (Vodka martinis are nice, but they are called "vodka martinis." A "martini" is a drink made with gin.)

2. A dry martini does contain a small amount of dry vermouth. Some people think that an extra-dry martini does not contain any vermouth. Wrong. If there is no vermouth, you're drinking chilled gin. Not a martini.

3. Purists insist that a proper martini is stirred, not shaken a la James Bond, because the ice is meant to chill the gin, not dilute it. Shaking breaks off lots of little ice shards that can water down the martini. This is a rule I often choose to ignore. Shaking is fun!

Fill a mixing glass or shaker with ice.

Add approximately 3½ ounces of gin (about 2 small shot glasses' worth).

Add a teaspoon of dry vermouth.

Stir or shake until chilled.

Strain into a chilled glass.

Add a lemon twist or a pimento-free olive. (Either add one olive or three, not two. Some say it's bad luck.)

Now, if you'd like a dry martini, you would pour the vermouth over the ice *before* adding the gin. Then, you would strain it back out, down the drain. Just enough vermouth adheres to the ice to flavor the martini without overpowering it.

THE GIBSON

A Gibson is a martini garnished with cocktail onions. Prepare as above, but instead of olives or a twist, add onions. Easy.

THE GIMLET

The best gimlets are made with fresh lime juice.

Fill a cocktail shaker with ice. Add a good swig of gin and the juice of half a lime and a dash of simple syrup.

Strain into a chilled martini glass and garnish with a lime wedge.

HOW TO MAKE SIMPLE SYRUP

In a small saucepan, bring 1 cup of sugar and 1 cup of water to a boil.

Stir until all the sugar is dissolved.

Remove from the heat and let cool completely.

Simple syrup won't go bad if kept in the refrigerator in a sealed jar.

It's also great for sweetening iced tea in the summer!

VODKA

People will add vodka to just about anything. If you're ever at a party where vodka-infused gummi worms are served, get the hell out of there as soon as possible. These people are amateurs. For vodka martinis, Gibsons, gimlets, or vodka tonics, follow the directions for their gin counterparts. Here are my recipes for other delicious vodka basics:

GREYHOUND

These are particularly nice when served before noon on weekends, as a little "hair of the dog."

Fill a tumbler with ice.

Add a hearty shot of vodka.

Fill the tumbler with freshly squeezed grapefruit juice.

SCREWDRIVER

Fill a tumbler with ice.

Add a hearty shot of vodka.

Fill the tumbler with freshly squeezed orange juice.

Garnish with a slice of orange.

BLOODY MARY

Fill a tall glass with ice.

Add a hearty shot of vodka.

Fill the glass three-quarters of the way with tomato juice.

Add about ½ teaspoon of horseradish, a squeeze of lemon, some freshly ground black pepper, a dash of Worcestershire sauce, and a dash of Tabasco.

Garnish with the traditional celery stalk. (I'm not a celery fan, so I garnish mine with a slice of cucumber.)

Sip while you wait for the pain to go away.

VODKA STINGER

My all-time favorite Broadway musical is *Company* by Stephen Sondheim and George Firth. In it, the character of Joanne, originally played by the inimitable Elaine Stritch, sings "The Ladies Who Lunch" and drinks vodka stingers like there's no tomorrow. Because of this, vodka stingers are fabulous.

Fill a tumbler with ice.

Add vodka.

Add an equal part of crème de menthe.

Ask your friend Bobby when you're gonna "make it." (That's a private joke for theater queens.)

TEQUILA

Tequila, as far as I'm concerned, should only be drunk as a shot or in a margarita. And while I have discovered through vigorous research that the more expensive the tequila the lesser the hangover, I can also tell you that any night that begins with tequila shots will inevitably end badly. Nevertheless . . .

TEQUILA SHOT

Cut a lemon into small wedges.

Pour tequila shots for you and your friends.

Lick one of your hands, right between your thumb and index finger. Apply salt before the spit dries.

Hold a wedge of lemon between your thumb and index finger of that same hand. Have your friends do the same.

Hold the tequila shot in the opposite hand.

Now, lick the salt.

Do the shot. Swallow.

Suck the lemon.

Watch the evening go downhill fast.

THE MARGARITA

At any given time, there are about 5,000 recipes for margaritas floating around. This one's the best.

Fill a shaker with ice.

Add a hearty shot of tequila.

Add a splash of Cointreau or Grand Marnier.

Add the juice of half a lime and a quick pour of simple syrup.

Shake and strain into a salt-rimmed glass. Or just serve on the rocks.

Garnish with a wedge of lime.

HOW TO SALT A RIM

Pour a layer of kosher salt onto a plate.
Run a wedge of lemon around the rim of a glass.
Turn the glass upside down and dip it into the salt.

BOURBON

Bourbon is a type of whiskey that is only made in America from at least 51% corn. In that regard, it differs from Scotch and Irish whiskeys, which are made from malted barley. Rye whiskey is made from—you guessed it—rye. There's a helluva lot more you could learn on the subject of whiskeys, but you're not gonna learn it here. All you need to know is that good bourbon is delicious.

THE MANHATTAN

Fill a shaker with ice.

Add a hearty shot of bourbon.

Add a splash of sweet vermouth and a dash of bitters.

You can also add a few drops of maraschino cherry juice, whatever that stuff is.

Shake and strain into a martini glass, and garnish with a maraschino cherry. If you're lazy, or alone, just drink it on the rocks.

IRISH WHISKEY

There's a bar in San Francisco called The Buena Vista, at the end of Hyde Street, right across from the cable-car platform in Fisherman's Wharf. I highly recommend you stop in for the best Irish coffee you can find.

Inspired by them, I make these at home for guests on cold winter's nights. In my family, we joke that they contain the four most important food groups: alcohol, sugar, fat, and caffeine.

IRISH COFFEE

In a glass mug, combine 2 teaspoons of sugar and some hot, freshly brewed coffee.

Leave about an inch at the top. Stir to dissolve the sugar.

Add a hearty shot of whiskey.

On top, float a thin layer of runny whipped cream. (If you pour the cream onto the back of a spoon held over the coffee mug, the cream will just float on top and not mix into the coffee.)

Note: You don't have to use fully whipped cream or add any sugar or vanilla to it. I like to fill a cocktail shaker with cold whipping cream and shake it until it just starts to get thick.

WINE

Let's move on to wine, one of life's great joys.

Disclaimer to any oenophiles who might be reading this: I am well aware that the complexities of wine cannot be fully explained within a few pages. The following list includes the most common characteristics of the most popular varieties and has been included in this book as a jumping-off point, if you will, for anyone who would like to begin learning more about wine. It should also be noted that wine snobbery actually diminishes your fabulousness quotient, especially when at a table full of people who are not wine aficionados you say things like, "Everyone knows 1991 was a dreadful year for Burgundy. It would absolutely ruin my weekend if you ordered a bottle." Your friends will not be impressed. They will think you're a douche.

Vin Blanc

WHITE WINE CHEAT SHEET

WINE	WHERE IT'S PRODUCED:	HOW IT TASTES:
CHABLIS	Various locations, especially France, in the Burgundy region	Dry, light, mineraly, steely, often with hints of vanilla or fruit
CHARDONNAY	Various locations, especially California and France	For the most part, California Chardonnays are more powerful than French ones and can be described as creamy, smoky, nutty, buttery, and/or steely. They are generally complex wines, often with highlights of apple, melon, lemon, or pineapple—and frequently, oak. Note: Chardonnay has become the most popular white wine, which accounts for its wide planting throughout the world.
CHENIN BLANC	Various locations, especially California and France in the Loire Valley	Crisp and balanced, hints of apple, pear, and pineapple
GEWÜRZTRAMINER	Various locations, especially Germany and France	Crispy, spicy, golden, floral aromas; can range from sweet to dry
PINOT BLANC	Various locations, especially California, Italy, and Alsace, France	Fresh, appley, a bit of spice and honey
PINOT GRIGIO	Various locations, especially Italy	Can range from very light and crisp to rich, full, and mineraly, with notes of honey or citrus Note: Pinot Grigio is basically the same wine as Pinot Gris, yet the Italian version has some different characteristics due to the different styles of winemaking.

WINE	WHERE IT'S PRODUCED:	HOW IT TASTES:
PINOT GRIS	Various locations, especially Alsace, France, and now Oregon	Crisp, light, dry, a bit flowery
POUILLY-FUMÉ	France, in the Loire Valley	Smoky (the word *fumé* means smoky in French), crisp, tart, and grassy Note: Sauvignon Blanc grapes are used to make Pouilly-Fumé. If you like this wine, you're likely to enjoy a Sancerre as well, which is also made with the same grape.
RIESLING	Various locations, especially Germany and the Alsace region of France	Delicate, fruity, spicy, complex, flower-scented; can range from dry to sweet Note: Generally speaking, German Rieslings are sweeter than their French counterparts.
SANCERRE	France, Loire Valley	Crisp, semidry, acidic, often with fruit or vegetable notes Note: The Sauvignon Blanc grape is used to produce Sancerre whites. A few Sancerre reds and rosés exist, but the region is really known for its whites.
SAUVIGNON BLANC	Various locations including France, California, New Zealand, South Africa	Crisp and dry with hints of grass and tropical fruit Note: New Zealand has become a leader in the production of some great Sauvignon Blancs, which are bottled with screw-cap tops. Some people say this lessens the "experience" of wine drinking. I disagree. Just pass the bottle and shut up.

Vino Rosso

RED WINE CHEAT SHEET

WINE	WHERE IT'S PRODUCED:	HOW IT TASTES:
BARBERA	Italy	Deep, full-bodied, notes of currant, high in acid Note: Barbera is generally a good all-purpose Italian red. It's not particularly fancy but goes well with pizza or a red sauce.
BAROLO	Italy	Rich, full, complex, earthy, high in alcohol Note: Because of its complexity and history as a favorite with the royal families of Europe, Barolo is considered the "wine of kings and the king of wines." Therefore, wine snobs love to extol its virtues or bash the hell out of it. Take it from me: Avoid getting embroiled in such banter until you really have an opinion.
BEAUJOLAIS	France, in part of the Burgundy region	Light, fruity, low in tannins, easy to drink Note: Most Burgundy reds are made from the Pinot Noir grape, but Beaujolais is made from the Gamay grape. Beaujolais is meant to be drunk while it's very young, so it's not a very complex wine. Around the world, the third Thursday of November is "Beaujolais Nouveau Day," when the newest batch of Beaujolais Nouveau is officially allowed to be consumed. Oh, the French.
BORDEAUX	France	Smoky, with notes of dark berries and wood; usually deep red in color Note: A red Bordeaux is usually a blend of grapes, including Cabernet Sauvignon, Cabernet Franc, and Merlot. While some of the world's most expensive wines are Bordeaux (Château Margeaux, Château Lafite-Rothschild, and Château Latour), you can also find many moderately priced ones.
CABERNET SAUVIGNON	Many varied locations (Cabernet is considered one of the world's most durable wines)	It can range from fairly mellow to very rich. Black currants are often a dominant flavor, sometimes with hints of oak and vanilla. Note: I could fill this book with all the different varieties of Cabernet Sauvignon, but I've got other stuff to talk about. Get a bottle and start drinking.

WINE	WHERE IT'S PRODUCED:	HOW IT TASTES:
CHIANTI	Italy	Strong, dry, bold Note: Wines labeled Chianti Classico, which usually have a black rooster on the label, are from a specific region of Italy between Florence and Siena and are generally known to be better quality. *Reserva* means the wine has been aged for three years total and at least one year in oak; *Gran Reserva* means it's been aged two years in oak and three in the bottle.
CÔTES DU RHÔNE	Rhône, France	Mostly mellow, some are fruitier than others; usually very drinkable
MALBEC	Various locations, especially Chile, Argentina, and France	Rustic, dark colored, medium- to full-bodied
MERLOT	Various locations	Complex, mellow, full, and fruity with dark fruit flavors of cherry, plum, and black currant Note: In France, Merlot is often used as a blending grape, whereas pure Merlots are common in California, Washington, and Chile.
PINOT NOIR	Various locations, especially France, California, Oregon	Earthy and often a bit like raspberry or plum jam when it's young; can be complex and smoky when older
RIOJA	Spain	Medium-bodied, often oaky with hints of vanilla Note: You've probably seen footage of the Battala del Vino (Battle of Wine) in Spain, where crazy Spaniards throw wine at one another for about three hours. The festival takes place in this region every June 29.
SANGIOVESE	Italy	Fresh and earthy, high acidity
SHIRAZ/SYRAH	Various locations, especially Australia and Rhône, France	Strong, spicy, with dark fruits and often a bit smoky
VALPOLICELLA	Italy	Light, fragrant, fruity
ZINFANDEL	California	Deep red, peppery, spicy, hints of fruit Note: This is one of the few wines that is known as a distinctly American variety and is often paired with American fare, like burgers and pizza.

HOW TO ORDER WINE IN A RESTAURANT

Sometimes you'll be presented with a wine list that might as well be written in Swahili. If so, don't get down on yourself; it happens to the most fabulous of us. I find this happens most often in upscale Italian restaurants because Italian wines aren't my specialty. Don't tell anyone I told you that. Most people think I'm perfect.

- If you don't recognize anything on the wine list, ask your waiter or wine steward for help. There's no shame in it; that's what he or she is there for.
- If you don't know what you want, know what you like. Mention some wines you've had in the past that you know you liked.
- Decide what you want to eat. A good server can help you choose something to complement what you're eating.
- If you're ordering by the glass, feel free to ask for a taste. Servers in good restaurants are happy to give you a free swig if the bottle is already open.
- When the wine arrives, check the label to make sure it's the wine you requested; make note, in particular, of whether it's the correct year.
- Don't sniff the cork! But feel free to give it a good squeeze. You're checking to make sure the cork is moist and not crumbly. A dehydrated cork means that the bottle was probably stored improperly. A dry cork lets air into the bottle, which can turn wine into vinegar.
- After the server pours a bit of wine in your glass, raise it up and swirl it around a bit. Check the color. It should be clear and not cloudy.

- Take a sip and let the server know if it's OK. He or she won't serve the rest of the table until you give your nod of approval or a simple "thank you."
- If you think the wine might have turned bad, ask your server to have a sip. In better restaurants, he or she will know how the wine is supposed to taste, but keep in mind that some wines have more acidic tastes than others.
- If you *really* don't like the wine, you're within your rights to send it back. However, if there's nothing actually wrong with the bottle, you probably shouldn't. Just chalk it up to experience and order something else.

HOW TO SERVE WINE AT HOME

- Stemmed glasses that are clear are preferable to colored glasses. Part of understanding and enjoying your wine is in being able to take in its color.
- Red wine should always be served in a glass with a large bowl, which allows it to breathe and allows you to swirl it around in the glass to open it up.
- White wine should be served in a glass with a smaller bowl and chilled. (Reds, with few exceptions, are at room temperature.)
- Remove the foil first and then insert the corkscrew as far as it will go; pull out the cork.
- The bottle should never touch the glass when being poured.
- A small amount should be poured first to allow for tasting. Only after the taster has approved the wine are the guests served. Serve the other guests first, saving the taster for last.

PAIRING FOOD AND WINE

This can be complicated, but one of the best and easiest ways to approach the question is to consider the weight of what you're eating and drinking. Heavy food needs an equally heavy or full-bodied wine to stand up to it. Conversely, light food will be overpowered by a wine that is too robust and calls for an equally light wine.

Use this chart to help you match the right wine with the right meal.

WHITE WINES		FOOD		RED WINES
CHABLIS PINOT BLANC RIESLING	LIGHT	Salads		
		Vegetables		
		White fish, *such as sole*		
PINOT GRIGIO PINOT GRIS CHAMPAGNES SPARKLING WINES	LIGHT- TO MEDIUM-BODIED	Sushi and fish tartares		
		Most shellfish, *including crab, mussels, shrimp, oysters*	LIGHT-BODIED	BEAUJOLAIS, RED BURGUNDY VALPOLICELLA
		Chicken, Turkey		
CHENIN BLANC CHABLIS GEWÜRZTRAMINER POUILLY-FUMÉ SANCERRE	MEDIUM-BODIED	Duck	LIGHT- TO MEDIUM-BODIED	BARBERA CHIANTI RIOJA
		Light pastas		
		Lobster		
		Stronger fish, *including, bass, salmon, tuna, swordfish*	MEDIUM-BODIED	CHIANTI CLASSICO, CÔTES DU RHÔNE MONTEPULCIANO, PINOT NOIR RIOJA RISERVA,SANGIOVESE
CHARDONNAY	MEDIUM- TO FULL-BODIED	Pork, Ham		
		Veal		
		Pizza	MEDIUM- TO FULL-BODIED	CABERNET SAUVIGNON MERLOT SHIRAZ
WHITE BORDEAUX SÉMILLON/CHARDONNAY BLENDS	FULL-BODIED	Heavy pastas		
		Steak tartare		
		Veal chops, Boar, Lamb		
		Steak	FULL-BODIED	BAROLO BORDEAUX MALBEC ZINFANDEL
		Venison		
		Roasts		
		Meatloaf, Burgers		

HOW TO
ENTERTAIN

WELCOME

In general, I'd rather throw a party than attend a party, mostly because I really get off on people telling me what a fabulous host I am. Honestly, how could I tire of hearing over and over and over, "Well, don't you look handsome . . . the hors d'oeuvres are delicious . . . the apartment looks gorgeous . . . how do you do it?"

It's amazing that with the constant praise, I'm as down-to-earth as I am.

I will admit that entertaining isn't always easy. However, to be a good host, you MUST foster the impression that, for you, entertaining requires less effort than picking up the phone to order some Kung Pao chicken. A frazzled host produces uneasy guests. And a host who talks about slaving away in the kitchen for three days prior to a party is a big ole bore. Believe me, your guests will be more relaxed, jovial, and engaging if you give them the impression you threw together a cocktail party for 50 people in half an hour. Nobody in their right mind would actually believe it, but the more effortless your attitude, the more comfortable and at home your guests will feel.

PLANNING

A successful party requires planning. You can't just invite a bunch of people over and hope for the best, as you may have done in college. You have to do some math. Yes, math. Here are some magic numbers to keep in mind when planning your next shindig:

People need about 4 to 5 feet of personal space during a cocktail party. So, if your unfurnished living room is 400 square feet, you can accommodate 80 to 100 people.

In general, about 80% of invited guests will RSVP in the affirmative. Of those people, 5% will flake out and not show up. So in general, for every 100 people you invite, plan on 75 attending.

Take it from me: Always hire a bartender for parties of 30 or more, otherwise you will spend the entire evening serving drinks. If your friends like the sauce as much as mine, hire a bartender for more than 20 people.

If you're not serving dinner, expect that each person will eat 10 appetizers over the course of the evening. If they know dinner is coming, your guests will eat about 6 each.

For a cocktail party, people consume about 2 drinks each for the first hour or so and then about 1 drink per hour after that (4 hours = 5 drinks per person).

You can get about 16 drinks out of your basic 750-ml bottle of liquor.

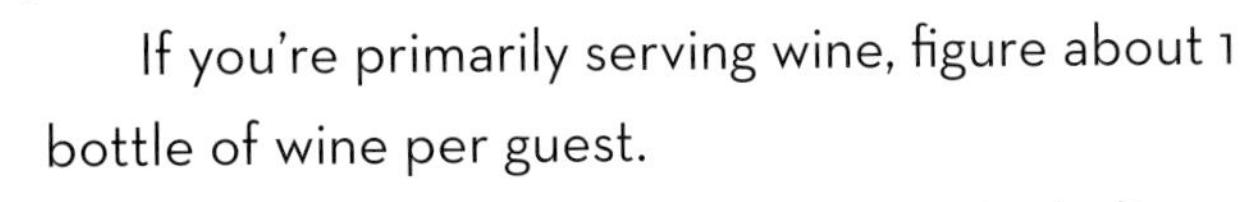

If you're primarily serving wine, figure about 1 bottle of wine per guest.

Figure about 1 quart mixer or nonalcoholic drink per person, which includes tonic, club soda, ginger ale, and sodas.

You'll need about 1 pound of ice cubes per person for an indoor party, and 2 pounds per person if it's an outdoor party in warm weather.

GIMME THE KEYS

Don't be a schmuck. If one of your guests is drunk, do not let him or her drive home. A good host protects his friends—and himself from lawsuits—by inflating the air mattress when necessary. Sometimes when I throw a party, I'll invite a do-gooder acquaintance who doesn't drink. You know, the type that likes to save other people from themselves. This type comes in very handy as the impromptu designated driver, even if he or she is not necessarily the life of the party.

THE LOO

When throwing a party, you must sanitize and guest-proof your bathroom. If the bathroom that will be used by your guests is not absolutely spotless, you will quickly get a reputation as a dirty birdy. And then, nobody will eat the food you've made because they're afraid of catching hepatitis.

You must also consider the contents of your medicine cabinet, because you cannot count on even your closest friends honoring your right to privacy. In fact, you should pretty much expect their curiosity to get the best of them, especially if you've been known to brag about how easily your doctor prescribes Xanax. In other words, hide the good stuff.

Knowing my friends' propensity for snooping, I enjoy playing a little trick, which I'll pass on to you: Get yourself a couple of marbles and place them precariously in the medicine cabinet so that the first person who opens it gets a

little surprise. That little *boink-boink-boink* off the counter and onto the tile floor is enough to embarrass the crap out of your nosiest guest.

OTHER BATHROOM ESSENTIALS

- **A SCENTED CANDLE.** Just in case—God forbid—someone makes a doodie.
- **PAPER HAND TOWELS.** Nobody wants to use the same terry-cloth towel as that guy who made a doodie.
- **HAND SOAP IN A PUMP.** People don't like sharing bar soap.
- **A WASTE CAN,** preferably with a foot-activated lid, so the used paper towels aren't visible.
- **EXTRA TOILET PAPER.** Put it under the sink so your guests can find it if necessary.
- **SPRAY CLEANER.** Also leave this under the sink just in case you need to do a little mid-party tidying up, which you should be doing about every hour. Being seen carrying the Fantastik from the kitchen is just not fabulous.

MUSIC

The right tunes are crucial to a party's success. In this age of MP3 players and iPods, there is absolutely no excuse for awkward silence. Take an hour or so to create a playlist designed specifically for your shindig, keeping in mind that classical music only works at dinner parties, and cocktail parties require more upbeat songs. I always enjoy a little "trip through the decades," dedicating the first hour or so to the '70s, the next to the '80s, then the '90s, and then some of the '00s. You know, maybe a little Olivia Newton-John ("Have You Never Been Mellow"), followed by Madonna ("Lucky Star"), Sir Mix-a-Lot ("Baby Got Back"), and Britney Spears ("Toxic"). This will make your guests feel their age. Older people always arrive first anyway, so they'll be happy to hear some of the stuff that was recorded before your younger guests were born.

As more people arrive, turn up the volume. People should have to speak at full voice but not scream to be heard.

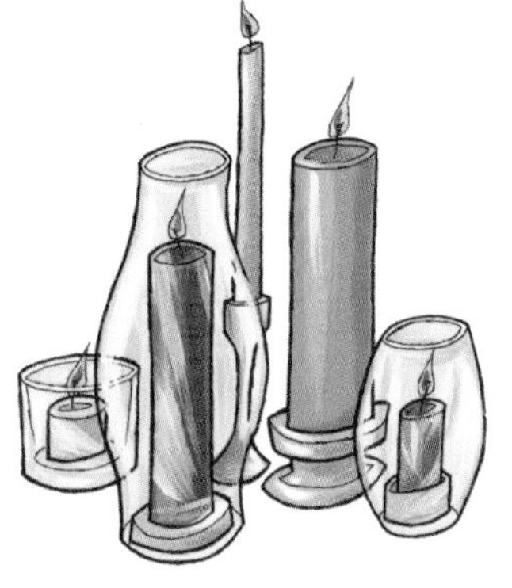

LIGHTING

Never have overhead lighting at a party; it makes everyone look old and tired. Candlelight is generally the most flattering light. Just be sure to place them in low-traffic areas. My friend Kelly almost went up in an angora blaze because I put a few votives on a credenza.

CIRCULATING

When you're hosting a party of more than 20 people, do not expect to have any sort of meaningful conversation with your guests. In fact, if you do, I consider you a failure. See, a meaningful conversation requires at least 20 minutes of your time. That's one-third of an hour, which means that during a four-hour party you could only have 12 meaningful conversations. What about the other eight people? You've ignored them and now they don't want to come to any of your parties. Besides, who's going to make sure all the hors d'oeuvres look pretty and there's plenty of ice?

A good guest knows that your time with her will be superficial but fabulous. Don't ask questions like, "What do you think of our foreign policy regarding the Middle East?" Instead, inquire, "Who is doing your hair these days? That cut really suits your heart-shaped face." Or whisper in someone's ear, "Don't tell anyone else I told you this, but if I were to swing both ways, I'd be all over you like Issey Miyake on an Olsen twin."

Your guest will feel special and you can attend to the rumaki.

MAKING PEOPLE FEEL COMFORTABLE

It's always awkward when someone shows up on time to your party. That's why I always wait until my first guest arrives to assemble at least one simple canapé. Then, I put that guest to work.

I'll say, "Meredith! Thank God you're here. I'm running so late. Would you be a dear and help me with these endive BLTs? Go wash your hands and roll up your sleeves. People will be here any minute." Now, instead of having to make conversation, you get a free catering assistant.

Besides providing food, drink, and music, your job as a host is to facilitate social networking—perhaps even a one-night stand. You must introduce people who do not already know each other, and the best way to do so is by finding a common bond, however lame it

seems: "Jim, have you met Sara? She also collects shells." "Fred, do you know Jerry? I've almost been arrested with each of you. Discuss." "Charlene, do you know Keira? You've both dabbled in the occult."

If one of your guests has failed in three conversational setups, cut and run. Some people are just wallflowers and need professional help. Make a note not to invite them to anything else. Ever. Unless they don't drink . . . in which case they could make perfectly good designated drivers. In general, however, the nonfabulous will suck the fabulous out of you.

GETTING PEOPLE TO LEAVE

You should always put an end time on your invitations, but expect people to stay at least an hour later. Even so, there will always be a few people who just don't want to go home. They might be alcoholics, or lonely, or they could be trapped in an unhappy marriage. In any case, if you don't want your guests hanging around until sunrise, try these subtle clues:

STEP ONE. **Start loading the dishwasher.**

STEP TWO. **Extinguish candles when people aren't looking.**

STEP THREE. **Hide the booze.**

STEP FOUR. **Talk about your day tomorrow.**

STEP FIVE. **Yawn.**

STEP SIX. **Go into the bedroom and call your home phone from your cell. Tell your guests it's your neighbor who's called the cops. Then say, "I hate to do this, but I really can't have The Fuzz stopping by twice in one week. They've already threatened to deport my cleaning lady and I couldn't live without her. But there's a great bar down the street if you're still thirsty!"**

HORS D'OEUVRES

Your party will be judged by the quality of your nibbly bits. That's just the way it goes, my friend. Here are my 25 favorites.

RUMAKI

I love chicken liver. (There, I said it—and I'm not ashamed!) I also love bacon because as everybody knows, it just makes life better. So essentially, these appetizers are little bundles of unconditional love on a toothpick.

Rumaki was popular in the '70s, so I've included this recipe in hopes that when you're eating it, you'll reflect fondly upon the days of polyester pantsuits and key parties.

Note: I use organic chicken livers when possible because the liver is, after all, the organ that filters out toxins. (Maybe that's too much information.) Enjoy!

YOU NEED:

¼ CUP SOY SAUCE

1 TEASPOON MINCED FRESH GINGER
(It wouldn't be the end of the world if you substituted some pickled ginger left over from take-out sushi.)

1 TEASPOON BROWN SUGAR

12 CHICKEN LIVERS, HALVED

12 WHOLE WATER CHESTNUTS, HALVED

ABOUT 4 SCALLIONS, GREEN PART ONLY, CUT INTO 1-INCH PIECES

12 SLICES BACON, CUT IN HALF CROSSWISE

24 TOOTHPICKS

Combine the soy sauce, ginger, and sugar in a bowl. Add the chicken livers and water chestnuts, and marinate for 30 minutes in the fridge. In a separate bowl, soak the toothpicks in some water (so they won't burn later).

After everything has marinated, wrap half a chicken liver, half a water chestnut, and a piece of scallion in half a slice of bacon and secure with a toothpick. Continue in this manner with the rest of the ingredients.

Place the rumaki on a broiler pan, and broil—not too close to the flame—until the bacon is crisp, turning once halfway through, about 10 to 15 minutes.

Serve hot.

"SWEDISH" MEATBALLS

I'll be honest. I'm including this one against my better judgment and with major apologies toward all Swedes. In fact, I'll extend that apology to Norwegians and Danes, just for good measure.

The following recipe is one that a certain family member of mine, who will remain nameless to protect her reputation, has been serving for almost 40 years. When I was a kid, I thought these were the most amazing things I had ever tasted in my life! Then, I asked for the recipe. "What!?!" I exclaimed upon reading it. "These should be called White Trash Balls!"

Nevertheless, I made them for a Christmas party a few years ago and served them alongside more upscale hors d'oeuvres to a room full of fancypants friends. Much to my surprise, these meatballs were the hit of the evening. My guests never knew the sauce is ketchup, sherry, and oregano. Suckahs!

YOU NEED:

1 POUND GROUND BEEF

½ CUP BREAD CRUMBS

¼ CUP MILK

1 TEASPOON MINCED ONION

½ TEASPOON SALT PLUS ADDITIONAL TO TASTE

2 TABLESPOONS BUTTER

¼ CUP SHERRY

¾ CUP KETCHUP

¼ TEASPOON OREGANO

In a bowl, combine the beef, bread crumbs, milk, onion, and salt. Mix well, then shape into small rounds.

Melt the butter in a large skillet over medium heat, and brown the meatballs in the butter. Pour off most of the fat. In a separate bowl, blend the sherry, ketchup, and oregano. Add salt to taste. Pour over the meatballs. Cover and simmer 20 minutes.

Pass the meatballs around on a platter while they're still warm or transfer them to a hot fondue pot if you want your guests to nibble.

(*Note:* I'll often form the meatballs and freeze them the night before. They'll keep their shape better while cooking, and it's one fewer thing to do on party day.)

SIRLOIN, CHEDDAR, AND CHUTNEY CROSTINI

This hearty, sweet, crunchy, savory gem is based on my all-time favorite sandwich in the world: roast beef with sharp cheddar and mango chutney on crusty French bread. Mmmmm. (I'm fancy, right?) It' actually a sandwich that was served in a Boston restaurant where I waited tables during college. That job is not to be confused with the singing waiter position I held for a short time on a Boston Harbor dinner cruise ship. Yes, that is correct: I once sang show tunes while serving clam chowder to tourists. But look at me now, people! There's hope for you, too.

YOU NEED:

1 POUND SIRLOIN STEAK

SALT AND PEPPER

1 LOAF FRENCH BREAD

OLIVE OIL

COARSE SALT

1 JAR MANGO CHUTNEY (YOU CAN FIND IT IN SPECIALTY STORES OR ONLINE)

ABOUT ¼ POUND SHARP CHEDDAR CHEESE

RED PEPPER FLAKES, OPTIONAL

Preheat the grill or broiler for 15 to 20 minutes.

Sprinkle the steak with salt and pepper, then grill or broil it to rare or medium-rare, depending on your preference. Let the steak rest for an hour or so, to get the juices back into the meat.

While the meat is cooling, you can make your crostini. Slice the French bread diagonally into ½-inch pieces. Brush with olive oil and sprinkle with coarse salt. Put the bread on a cookie sheet, and place under the broiler until golden brown.

Spread a little mango chutney on each crostini, and top with a thin slice of sirloin and a thin slice of cheddar cheese. If you like things spicy, you can add some red pepper flakes on top of the chutney. Yum!

CUCUMBER SANDWICHES

My grandma Kona, who's an actual card-carrying member of The Daughters of the British Empire—I kid you not—will occasionally make these for afternoon tea. They're not fancy, but they're very civilized. I like to serve them when I invite just a few friends over for a glass of Champagne on a Saturday afternoon.

YOU NEED:

1 CUCUMBER, PEELED AND SLICED VERY THIN (I USE HOT-HOUSE SEEDLESS ONES)

½ CUP WATER

½ CUP WHITE VINEGAR

BUTTER, SOFTENED

SOME FANCY WHITE BREAD

FRESHLY GROUND BLACK PEPPER

After slicing the cucumber very thin (I bought a mandolin slicer just for this purpose), place the slices in a bowl with the water and vinegar. Let soak for about 15 minutes at room temperature.

Drain and dry the cucumber on a paper towel.

Butter the bread and arrange the cucumber slices on top. Sprinkle with pepper.

Top with another piece of bread. Remove the crusts, and cut the sandwiches into small squares, rectangles, or triangles. (They're shown here as open-faced sandwiches; otherwise they'd just look like pieces of bread.)

WATERMELON CUBES WITH FETA

These are awesome on a hot summer's day. The saltiness of the feta pairs perfectly with the sweet crunchiness of the watermelon, and the lime adds a hint of citrus . . . but mainly just looks pretty. You can serve individual skewers or lightly toss together as a simple salad, with some very light olive oil and torn mint leaves.

YOU NEED:

1 LIME, CUT INTO SMALL SLICES

1 SMALL SEEDLESS WATERMELON, CUT INTO SMALL CUBES

1 BLOCK OF FETA CHEESE, CUT INTO SAME-SIZE CUBES

Cut and cube the stuff, skewer it, and serve it. Simple as that!

SHRIMP DE JONG

Serve your guests shrimp whenever possible. It's a guaranteed crowd pleaser.

Foodies may have heard of "shrimp de jonghe," which is a casserole created by De Jonghe's Hotel and Restaurant in Chicago almost 100 years ago. I've put my own little twist on it, and I tell people that Erica Jong gave me the recipe. Some of my friends have taken to calling it That Feminist Shrimp.

I've never met Erica Jong, and I have no idea if she even eats shrimp. But if you're reading this, Erica, you're invited over whenever you want!

YOU NEED:

1½ STICKS (¾ CUP) SALTED BUTTER, SOFTENED

1 CUP BREAD CRUMBS

2 TABLESPOONS FLAT-LEAF PARSLEY, COARSELY CHOPPED

½ CUP DRY SHERRY

4 CLOVES GARLIC, MINCED

1 TABLESPOON CAPERS, DRAINED BUT NOT RINSED

1 TEASPOON SALT

1 TEASPOON PEPPER

2 POUNDS LARGE SHRIMP, SHELLED AND DEVEINED

JUICE OF 1 LEMON

Preheat the oven to 375°F.

In a bowl, stir together the butter, bread crumbs, parsley, sherry, garlic, capers, salt, and pepper until blended.

Layer the shrimp in a shallow casserole dish and top with the bread-crumb mixture.

Bake for about 30 minutes—stirring once or twice during cooking—until the shrimp turn pink and the bread crumbs get all toasty looking.

Sprinkle with fresh lemon juice and serve hot.

TUNA TARTARE WITH WONTON CHIPS

I only pull this one out for people I really like. And I make sure they eat it while it's still cold and fresh. By the end of the night (if there's any left), you won't want to go near this stuff without a hazmat suit.

Get the freshest tuna you can find for this. If you can buy toro (the tuna belly), even better. You can chop everything a few hours beforehand and keep the tuna in the refrigerator, but don't combine the ingredients until the party starts. Feel free to substitute a high-quality potato chip for the wonton crisps. I like the ones with sea salt on them.

YOU NEED:

For the tuna tartare:

1 POUND SUSHI-QUALITY TUNA, CUT INTO A SMALL DICE

1 AVOCADO, DICED

1/8 CUP CANOLA OIL

1/2 TEASPOON PEELED AND FINELY GRATED GINGER

1 TEASPOON FINELY CHOPPED JALAPEÑO

1 TEASPOON WASABI POWDER
(You can find this in the Asian section of your supermarket or you can ask your local sushi restaurant for some.)

1 SCALLION, GREEN AND WHITE PARTS, FINELY DICED

BLACK SESAME SEEDS

SALT AND PEPPER TO TASTE

For the wonton chips:

18 OR SO SQUARE WONTON WRAPPERS

VEGETABLE OIL OR MELTED BUTTER

SEA SALT OR SESAME SEEDS

FOR THE TUNA TARTARE:

When dicing the tuna, be sure to use a very clean cutting board and a very sharp knife. Discard any part of the tuna filet that's dark (bloody) or stringy (nerves). I work with about 1/4 pound at a time, keeping the remainder in the refrigerator. You can keep the tuna in a large mixing bowl covered with plastic wrap until you're ready to add the other ingredients.

Have everything else chopped, diced, and measured out when your guests arrive, so that you can combine it all at the last minute and serve it super-fresh.

I know this seems like a lot of work, but it's delish. You could even serve it as a first course for a dinner party on individual plates, perhaps over some mild mixed greens.

FOR THE WONTON CHIPS:

Cut the wanton wrappers in half diagonally, and arrange them on a cookie sheet. Spray with vegetable oil or brush lightly with melted butter. Top with sea salt or sesame seeds. Bake at 350°F for a few minutes until golden brown and crisp.

TAPENADE THREEWAY

It's practically a law that you must serve olives at a cocktail party. This probably has something to do with the saltiness of the olives making you want more liquor. Every once in a while, I like to mix it up a bit and serve black-olive and green-olive tapenade instead of whole olives. Yeah, I'm crazy like that.

I also like to serve sun-dried tomato tapenade, as it complements both the black- and green-olive tapenade nicely. Making tapenade is a breeze if you own a food processor—especially one of those mini ones. If not, you can use a mortar and pestle. But I have to be honest, that seems like a lot of freakin' work.

You can serve these tapenades separately with some nice crackers or crostini. Or you could go to town and combine all three on a crostini.

YOU NEED:

For the black-olive tapenade:

½ POUND GOOD-QUALITY BLACK OLIVES, PITTED AND DRAINED

4 ANCHOVY FILLETS

1 CLOVE GARLIC, PEELED

4 TABLESPOONS OLIVE OIL

Put all of the ingredients (except the olive oil) into a food processor. Pulse a few times to combine, then add the oil tablespoon by tablespoon until a slightly chunky consistency is achieved.

For the green-olive tapenade:

½ POUND GOOD-QUALITY GREEN OLIVES, PITTED AND DRAINED

2 TABLESPOONS CAPERS, DRAINED

1 CLOVE GARLIC, PEELED

1 TEASPOON FRESH LEMON JUICE

4 TABLESPOONS OLIVE OIL

Put all of the ingredients (except the olive oil) into a food processor. Pulse a few times to combine, then add the oil tablespoon by tablespoon until a slightly chunky consistency is achieved.

For the sun-dried tomato tapenade:

½ CUP SUN-DRIED TOMATOES, DRAINED

2 CLOVES GARLIC, PEELED

¼ TEASPOON SALT

6 LEAVES FRESH BASIL, CHOPPED

3 TABLESPOONS OLIVE OIL

Put all of the ingredients (except the olive oil) into a food processor. Pulse a few times to combine, then add the oil tablespoon by tablespoon until a slightly chunky consistency is achieved.

These can be made a couple of days in advance if stored covered in the fridge.

LOBSTER SALAD ON CUCUMBER SLICES

After a few summer trips to Maine in search of the perfect lobster roll, I've become a purist of sorts. My favorite roll comes from a place in Cape Porpoise that uses only fresh lobster meat and Hellmann's mayonnaise. So that's how I make my lobster salad. Except I use frozen lobster meat and add a little diced yellow pepper for some crunch and color. Oh, and I add salt and pepper. I guess my lobster salad isn't quite like theirs after all.

You can make the lobster salad earlier in the day and keep it covered in the refrigerator. And you might as well slice the cukes while you're at it and keep them in the fridge separately. Assemble just before your guests arrive.

YOU NEED:

1 OR 2 CUCUMBERS, DEPENDING ON THEIR SIZE

1 POUND FROZEN LOBSTER MEAT, THAWED AND DRAINED

½ CUP MAYONNAISE

¼ CUP FINELY DICED YELLOW PEPPER

SALT AND PEPPER TO TASTE

Peel and slice the cucumber into ⅛-inch-thick slices. (They need to be a little thick to support the weight of the lobster salad.) Reserve in a bowl of cold water until you're ready to assemble the appetizers.

Chop the lobster meat into small pieces. Toss in a bowl with the mayo, yellow pepper, salt, and pepper.

Place a spoonful on each cucumber slice.

WILD MUSHROOM CROSTINI

This mushroom mixture is so delicious I could eat it by the bowlful. It's also pretty hard to screw up, which makes it a great option for anyone who doesn't cook much. You can even make it a day ahead and keep it refrigerated. Bring to room temperature before serving. A quick shot under the broiler will warm it up just enough.

YOU NEED:

1 TABLESPOON BUTTER

1 TABLESPOON OLIVE OIL PLUS ADDITIONAL FOR BRUSHING THE BREAD

¼ CUP CHOPPED SHALLOTS

1 CLOVE GARLIC, MINCED

1 TEASPOON MINCED FRESH ROSEMARY

5 CUPS ASSORTED WILD MUSHROOMS, CHOPPED

½ TEASPOON GRATED LEMON PEEL

¼ CUP WHIPPING CREAM

¾ CUP GRATED FONTINA CHEESE

¾ CUP GRATED ROMANO CHEESE

1 LOAF FRENCH BREAD

COARSE SALT

Add the butter and olive oil to a large pan over medium heat. When the butter melts, add the shallots, garlic, and rosemary, and sauté until the shallots are translucent. Don't let the garlic burn. Add the mushrooms, and sauté until browned and most of the liquid has evaporated.

Remove from the heat. Add the lemon peel, cream, and cheeses.

While the mixture is cooling, slice the French bread diagonally into ½-inch pieces. Brush with olive oil and sprinkle with coarse salt.

Spread the cooled mixture on the crostini. Place them on a baking sheet and place under the broiler until they get all bubbly and delicious-looking. Serve warm.

ENDIVE BLTS

One of my favorite things about making hors d'oeuvres is the challenge of shrinking a delicious meal down into a delicious bite-size morsel. And I love me a bacon, lettuce, and tomato sandwich. So I figured one evening, why not do it on endive? It's a lettuce!

You'll pardon me, I hope, if the recipe isn't precise. I never actually wrote it down. Besides, it's not exactly like assembling an Ikea bookshelf.

YOU NEED:

A BUNCH OF BACON

A FEW HEADS OF ENDIVE

A BUNCH OF CHERRY OR PEAR TOMATOES, HALVED

SPICY MAYONNAISE *(I add cayenne pepper to taste—or you could use a high-quality ranch or Thousand Island dressing.)*

Fry up the bacon, nice and crisp. When it cools, break the slices into manageable pieces. Cut the base off the endive heads and arrange the leaves on a platter.

On each leaf, place half a tomato and some mayonnaise or dressing. Keep nice and cold until ready to serve. Then top with a little bacon and make your friends happy.

ROASTED GARLIC TOASTS

If you've never tasted roasted garlic, you are in for a treat! It's buttery in texture and surprisingly sweet, with just a fraction of the garlicky taste. I had never had it until I worked in a restaurant in college that served whole bulbs roasted and served with slices of toasted Italian bread. Then I went through a phase where I had to have it every night. You can serve it at a dinner party as an appetizer in the bulb and let people spread it themselves, but for cocktail parties I do the spreading.

Check out how easy this is.

YOU NEED:

6 BULBS GARLIC

OLIVE OIL

SALT

SLICED ITALIAN BREAD, TOASTED

Preheat the oven to 375°F.

Cut the tops off the garlic bulbs so that the meat of the garlic cloves is exposed. Don't separate the bulb. Place the bulbs on a baking sheet, cut sides up.

Pour olive oil onto each bulb so that every clove gets a little. Sprinkle with salt. Cover with aluminum foil and bake for about an hour. Check after about 45 minutes. The garlic should be golden brown and mushy. Don't let it burn.

Let them cool a little, so that they're easy to handle.

Squeeze the entire bulb over a bowl to catch the goodness. Mix it all up and add salt to taste. Keep at room temperature and spread over thin, toasted slices of Italian bread.

CRAB-STUFFED MUSHROOMS

I once challenged my friend Kim Upham to an hors d'oeuvre-off. Even though I was the winner (I was the judge, jury, and appeals court), she placed a very close second. Her prize: Four of her best recipes would be featured in my book, but she would receive no monetary compensation. Second place sucks, doesn't it, Kimmers? I will, however, give her an autographed copy of this book—when it gets marked down and I get around to it.

YOU NEED:

2 TABLESPOONS OLIVE OIL PLUS ADDITIONAL FOR COATING THE MUSHROOMS

1 TABLESPOON BUTTER

3 SHALLOTS, FINELY CHOPPED

1 CUP SHREDDED COOKED CRABMEAT

1 TABLESPOON FINE, DRY, SEASONED BREAD CRUMBS

1 TABLESPOON CHOPPED GREEN ONION

1 TABLESPOON CHOPPED PARSLEY

1 TABLESPOON CHOPPED CHIVES

1 TEASPOON KOSHER SALT

½ TEASPOON CAYENNE PEPPER

⅛ TEASPOON GARLIC POWDER

BLACK PEPPER TO TASTE

4 TABLESPOONS GRATED PARMESAN CHEESE, DIVIDED IN HALF

1 EGG, SLIGHTLY BEATEN

24 BABY PORTOBELLO MUSHROOMS, CLEANED AND STEMS REMOVED

2 TABLESPOONS BUTTER, MELTED

JUICE OF 1 LEMON

Preheat the oven to 350°F.

Add the olive oil and butter to a small sauté pan over medium heat, and cook the shallots until caramelized, about 10 minutes.

In a bowl, combine the crabmeat, bread crumbs, onion, parsley, and chives. Add the spices and half of the Parmesan. Add the shallots and egg and mix well.

Lightly coat the mushroom caps with olive oil and arrange them on a nonstick baking sheet. Spoon the crab mixture into the mushrooms, mounding slightly. Sprinkle with the remaining Parmesan and additional bread crumbs if desired. Drizzle with the melted butter.

Bake for 20 minutes or until slightly browned. Squeeze lemon juice and add additional salt as desired.

SLIDERS WITH MANCHEGO AND SPICY KETCHUP

This is another one of Kim's. That girl can cook.

I'd serve these if I had a lot of straight guys coming over to watch football or talk about breasts.

YOU NEED:

For the sliders:

2 POUNDS GROUND SIRLOIN, 85% LEAN

2 POUNDS GROUND CHUCK, 85% LEAN

KOSHER SALT

BLACK PEPPER

24 POTATO DINNER ROLLS, SLICED IN HALF

2 TABLESPOONS BUTTER, MELTED

Preheat the oven to 350°F. On the stovetop, heat a cast-iron skillet to medium.

Mix the ground beef and make 24 patties, approximately 3 inches in diameter and 3/4-inches thick. Season generously with salt and pepper on both sides. Sauté the patties a few at a time, 4 to 5 minutes on each side for medium-rare. (Do not press the patties with a spatula or unnecessarily flip them; this dries them out.)

Brush the rolls with the melted butter and bake until just slightly toasted.

For the spicy ketchup:

2 TABLESPOONS OLIVE OIL

½ LARGE YELLOW ONION, CHOPPED

1 CLOVE GARLIC, CHOPPED

½ RED BELL PEPPER, SEEDED AND CHOPPED

1 JALAPEÑO, SEEDED AND FINELY CHOPPED

1 TOMATO, SEEDED AND CHOPPED

6 OUNCES KETCHUP

¼ CUP CILANTRO, CHOPPED

KOSHER SALT

BLACK PEPPER

½ POUND GRATED MANCHEGO CHEESE

Heat the olive oil to medium-high in a medium sauté pan. Cook the onion and garlic 2 to 3 minutes, then add the red pepper and cook another 3 to 4 minutes. Add the jalapeño, tomato, ketchup, cilantro, salt, and pepper. Simmer another 5 minutes to bring the flavors together.

When the patties are nearly done, top with the Manchego so the cheese melts. Then layer the patties on the potato rolls with the spicy ketchup.

DATE AND BLUE CHEESE BRUSCHETTA

Kim again. This may be my favorite of hers because it involves blue cheese and prosciutto. I mean, you could stuff an old sneaker with blue cheese and roll it in prosciutto and I'd eat it. But these require a lot less chewing.

YOU NEED:

1 LOAF FRENCH BREAD, SLICED INTO ½-INCH SLICES

EXTRA-VIRGIN OLIVE OIL

KOSHER SALT

BLACK PEPPER

8 OUNCES CRUMBLED BLUE CHEESE

12 DATES, CUT IN HALF WITH PITS REMOVED *(figs may be substituted if in season)*

4 OUNCES PROSCIUTTO

Preheat the oven to 350°F.

Brush the slices of bread on both sides with olive oil. Arrange the bread on a baking sheet and bake for 5 minutes, then turn the slices over and bake for another 5 minutes.

Remove the bread from the oven and turn the broiler to high.

Season the toasted bread with salt and pepper. Spoon just enough cheese to cover the bread, and place half a date on each slice. Broil the slices for 1 to 2 minutes until the cheese is melted and dates begin to caramelize. Remove from the oven, and layer a piece of prosciutto on each slice.

Serve warm.

SPICED SWEET POTATO FRIES WITH MASCARPONE DIP

This is the last one from Kim because I feel like she's starting to steal my spotlight. But I'd like to remind her:

YOU CAME IN SECOND! I AM THE KING OF HORS D'OEUVRES!!!

This recipe basically requires you to dump half your spice cabinet into a bowl. Or you could buy a seasoned spice blend. Whatever.

YOU NEED:

For the sweet potato fries:

4 SWEET POTATOES, HALVED CROSSWISE AND THEN SLICED INTO 8 WEDGES EACH

OLIVE OIL

1 TABLESPOON FLOUR

1 TEASPOON KOSHER SALT

1 TEASPOON GARLIC SALT

½ TEASPOON PAPRIKA

¼ TEASPOON CAYENNE PEPPER

¼ TEASPOON CHILI POWDER

¼ TEASPOON BLACK PEPPER

¼ TEASPOON CINNAMON

¼ TEASPOON CUMIN

¼ TEASPOON DRIED THYME

¼ TEASPOON DRIED OREGANO

Preheat the oven to 400°F.

Toss the potato wedges lightly with olive oil in a large bowl.

In a small bowl, mix the flour and all of the spices together. Toss the wedges with the spice mix, then arrange them in a single layer on a foil-lined baking sheet. Bake for 15 minutes, then remove from the oven, flip the potatoes, and bake for another 15 minutes, until the potato edges are crisp.

For the mascarpone dip:

½ CUP MASCARPONE CHEESE

½ CUP SOUR CREAM

1 TABLESPOON HONEY

Blend all of the ingredients and serve alongside the spiced wedges.

CRUNCHY, SWEET, AND CREAMY ENDIVES

These are really easy (you don't need an actual recipe) and they look really beautiful when arranged on a platter. And as an added bonus, they taste great—light but with a little heft because of the cheese.

Feel free to experiment with different types of cheeses and nuts depending on your personal tastes. I've found that a mild gorgonzola works nicely with toasted pine nuts.

YOU NEED:

2 OR 3 HEADS ENDIVE

SOME NICE GOAT CHEESE

SOME CANDIED WALNUTS
(My local specialty store sells them premade, but you can use just regular walnuts.)

SOME HONEY

Cut the bases off the endive to separate the leaves. Make a pretty arrangement on a platter. Sometimes I do them in neat rows. Other times I fan them out.

Top each leaf with a small dollop of goat cheese and some chopped walnuts.

Drizzle with delicious honey.

FOIE GRAS BRIOCHE

One of my favorite things in life is to sit outside at a café in Paris called Les Deux Magots and eat foie gras, drink beer, and watch the world go by. Oh, damn those French for being so effortlessly fabulous.

YOU NEED:

1 LOAF BRIOCHE OR CHALLAH BREAD

½ POUND PÂTÉ DE FOIE GRAS

SOME LINGONBERRY JAM

(*which is not French but Swedish—whatever*)

Cut the bread into ½-inch slices, discarding the crusts. Then shape them into pretty squares or triangles. Toast lightly. Take your nephews to the lake and let them feed the ducks any extra bread.

Give each toasted piece of bread a smear of the pâté and a dollop of jam. You can certainly omit the jam, but I like the sweet tartness. It also makes the appetizers a little prettier, because let's face it: foie gras is kind of flesh-colored. Not cute.

PROSCIUTTO FILLED WITH HAPPINESS

You'll want to scarf these little cornucopias down as fast as you can make them.

YOU NEED:

¼ CUP PINE NUTS

ABOUT 20 THIN SLICES OF GOOD-QUALITY PROSCIUTTO

1 SMALL BUNCH ARUGULA

¼ POUND GORGONZOLA

¼ CUP CURRANTS

Spread the pine nuts on a baking sheet and bake at 350°F until they turn golden brown. (I do mine in the toaster oven.) You'll want to keep a close eye on these because they go from golden brown to burned very quickly, as I've learned on three or four occasions. Transfer to a small bowl and let them cool.

Cut each slice of prosciutto in half, crosswise. Don't worry if they're not perfect. Top each half-slice with a small piece of arugula, a dab of gorgonzola, a few pine nuts, and a few currants. Then roll them into little mini-horns.

Arrange on a platter and serve.

SALMON MOUSSE ON PUMPERNICKEL

This one's a little fancy. Not too fancy. But fancy. And delicious. It's deliciously fancy, I guess. Or fancily delicious. Oh, whatever. Just try it!

YOU NEED:

- **2 BONELESS, 8-OUNCE SALMON FILETS**
- **1 ENVELOPE UNFLAVORED GELATIN**
- **2 TABLESPOONS COLD WATER**
- **½ CUP BOILING WATER**
- **½ CUP MAYONNAISE**
- **1 TABLESPOON FRESH LEMON JUICE**
- **1 TABLESPOON FINELY GRATED ONION**
- **2 DASHES OF HOT SAUCE, LIKE TABASCO**
- **1 TEASPOON SALT**
- **2 TABLESPOONS FINELY CHOPPED DILL**
- **1 CUP HEAVY CREAM**
- **1 CUCUMBER, PEELED, SEEDED, AND FINELY DICED**

I poach my own salmon for this, rather than use canned. It's really easy. Fill a large heavy skillet with enough water to cover the two salmon fillets. Bring the water to a boil, then reduce to a simmer.

Place the salmon fillets, skin side down, into the water and simmer, covered, for 8 minutes.

Note: If you are poaching the salmon fillets to be eaten alone or over greens, you can poach them in a broth of 50 percent white wine, 50 percent water, and season the broth with kosher salt, cracked peppercorns, and lemon slices.

When the salmon is done, remove from the liquid and place on a clean towel to drain and cool to room temperature. Then, remove the skin and flake the salmon into small pieces.

In a large mixing bowl, add the gelatin and the cold water. Stir to combine. Then add the boiling water and stir until the gelatin dissolves. Cool to room temperature.

Now add the flaked salmon, mayonnaise, lemon juice, onion, salt, dill and hot sauce. Stir to blend completely and refrigerate for about 20 minutes.

In a separate bowl, whip the cream until it is thickened to soft peaks. Fold gently into the salmon mixture.

Transfer the mixture to a nonstick decorative mold or glass bowl or baking dish lined with plastic wrap. Cover and chill for 4 hours.

Serve on pumpernickel toasts, no crusts. Top with some cucumber and dill sprigs.

LAMB DINNER ON CROSTINI

You've probably been to a cocktail party where they've served mini lamb chops with sauce. Delicious, right? But I don't like watching people gnaw on a bone. (Well, actually it's hot when some people do it but not most.) I also don't like people watching me while I gnaw on a bone. And most of all, I don't want to stand around with a half-eaten bone in my hand while I'm discussing the nuances of Nietzsche or the latest trashy reality show. Do the work for your guests!

YOU NEED:

6 LAMB CHOPS

OLIVE OIL

SALT AND PEPPER

1 PARSNIP, THINLY SLICED

ABOUT 24 SLICES ITALIAN BREAD, TOASTED

MINT JELLY

Lightly brush the lamb chops with olive oil, and salt and pepper them. Cook under the broiler until medium-rare (about 6 minutes per side). Let sit at room temperature.

Spread the parsnip slices on a baking sheet, and spray or brush them with olive oil. Season with salt and pepper. Bake at 350°F until crisp.

Arrange the crostini on a serving platter.

Cut each lamb loin off the bone, then thinly slice. Place some lamb on each crostini, and sprinkle with salt. Top with a small dollop of mint jelly and a parsnip crisp.

FINGERLING TREATS

You can assemble these for your guests, as shown. But I often serve the roasted potatoes (heavily salted and rosemaried) around a big bowl of crème fraîche or sour cream or even homemade mayonnaise. They're nice with some caviar also.

YOU NEED:

ABOUT 16 FINGERLING POTATOES, CUT IN HALF LENGTHWISE

OLIVE OIL

2 TABLESPOONS FINELY CHOPPED ROSEMARY

SALT AND PEPPER TO TASTE

½ CUP SOUR CREAM OR CRÈME FRAÎCHE

ROASTED RED PEPPERS, DICED

Place the potatoes in a large mixing bowl. Add enough olive oil to coat lightly, along with the rosemary and salt and pepper.

Place the potatoes, cut side down, on a baking sheet. Bake at 375°F for about 45 minutes until cooked through.

When the potatoes have fully cooled, top with a dollop of sour cream and some diced red peppers. Sprinkle with salt and pepper.

RADISH ADDICTION

When I was a kid, my sister and I would make a platter of these after school and eat them while watching *The Brady Bunch* and *Gilligan's Island*. To this day, I can tell you the plot of any episode just by watching the first two seconds. I can also still eat a whole platter of these. Granted, they're nothing fancy, but they're always the first things to go. Try them when you're inviting a few friends over for beer on a hot summer's day.

YOU NEED:

A COUPLE OF BAGS OF RADISHES

BUTTER, SOFTENED

KOSHER SALT

Slice off the tips of the radishes so that the bottoms are flat. (They won't roll off the platter that way.) With a small sharp knife, cut a cone-shaped opening in the top of each radish. Fill with softened butter and sprinkle with kosher salt.

That's it!

CHICKEN LIVER PÂTÉ

Some people are put off by the fact that chicken liver pâté looks a little like baby poop. Oh well, more for the rest of us!

YOU NEED:

2 TABLESPOONS OLIVE OIL

½ CUP FINELY CHOPPED YELLOW ONION

1 CLOVE GARLIC, MINCED

1 CUP CHICKEN LIVERS, FINELY CHOPPED

6 ANCHOVY FILLETS

2 TEASPOONS CHOPPED SAGE

¼ CUP SHERRY

½ TEASPOON SALT

½ TEASPOON PEPPER

Heat the olive oil over medium heat in a medium-size skillet. Add the onion and sauté until translucent. Add the garlic, chicken livers, anchovies, and sage. Stir until the liver is cooked through, about 10 minutes. Increase the heat to high, add the sherry, and cook for 3 more minutes. Add the salt and pepper. Remove from the heat and pulse in a food processor until blended. The final mixture should be a little chunky. Refrigerate and serve with crostini or crackers.

Hint: If your final mixture is too watery even after refrigerating, you can add a finely chopped hard-boiled egg to thicken it up.

MAC AND CHEESE WITH BACON!

Last year I started a New Year's Eve tradition: hot macaroni and cheese with bacon served at midnight! I mean, could you think of a better way to welcome the next 365 days? My guests and I were a little tipsy, so you can be sure not an elbow went to waste.

YOU NEED:

8 SLICES THICK-CUT BACON

2 CUPS ELBOW MACARONI *(dry)*

1 CUP WHIPPING CREAM

1 CUP WHOLE MILK

⅛ TEASPOON GROUND NUTMEG

6 OUNCES GRUYÈRE, GRATED

SALT AND FRESHLY GROUND PEPPER

4 TABLESPOONS GRATED PARMESAN CHEESE

Preheat the oven to 400°F.

Butter a medium-size baking dish.

Cook the bacon until crispy. Drain on paper towels. When cool, cut or break into small pieces.

Cook the macaroni until al dente. Drain well.

Mix the cream, milk, bacon, nutmeg, and about ⅓ of the Gruyère in a large bowl. Add the macaroni and mix. Taste, then season with salt and pepper. Transfer the macaroni mixture to the greased baking dish. Sprinkle the remaining Gruyère on top. Then sprinkle with the Parmesan. Bake for about 20 minutes.

Congratulations!

You now know how to entertain fabulously and are only one chapter away from being FREAKIN' FABULOUS!

HOW TO
DECORATE

Now that you know how to dress, behave, speak, eat, drink, and entertain fabulously, you must have a freakin' fabulous place in which to do it.

Your home should be a reflection of you at your very best. You're witty, colorful, neat, and stylish (at least that's how I choose to picture you), so your home should express those same qualities—pleasing the eye and generating good feelings.

Decorating fabulously means surrounding yourself with things that make you happy and that flatter you. By you, I mean one person. Decorating by committee will compromise your vision, so have a strategy ready. Let your significant other dictate what the outside of your house looks like, or what car to buy. But you should keep command over the interiors. If your cohabitant gives you any grief, point out the cost of attending therapy five days a week. Or you can throw a hissy fit and threaten to withhold sex. Works for me!

Again, your home is a reflection of you. If you're surrounded by dull, dingy décor, how can you expect to exude vibrant, fascinating fabulousness? As I stroll through my space, I want to feel invigorated by color, shapes, and textures. When I hit the bedroom, I want to feel calm and soothed. Except for those special 15 minutes per week.

Not to go all voodoo priest on you, but your house creates a vibe that impacts your entire day. Never underestimate the mojo of your environment. If my apartment's a mess, I'm a mess. If my place smiles serenely as I leave, I glide into the day. Get me? Good.

Let's begin with my **TOP THREE** Decorating Pitfalls and Fears:

1. WORRYING ABOUT RESALE VALUE

Ugh. Call me a throwback, but I believe the primary purpose of a home is to give you a delightful place to relax and entertain. Century 21 might preach neutrals, neutrals, neutrals. But that's for people who live in neutral. I live in third gear. Or sometimes reverse.

2. NOT TAKING CHANCES

For my living room in Connecticut, I wanted a six-foot antler chandelier. And I wanted it painted high-gloss black. Oh, the grief my contractors, my family, my friends gave me about that chandelier. "You'll regret it!" "You're messing with Mother Nature's handiwork!" Did I listen? No. That ebony masterpiece is freaky, and I l-o-v-e it. Does everybody agree? Nope.

If you are pleasing everybody, you're doing something wrong. How to tell you're on the right track? When your sister-in-law enters and says, "Oh . . . that's different." Success!

3. BELIEVING YOU CAN'T AFFORD IT

Fabulousness can be bought. If you have the dough to hire a decorator, do it. But if you're flat broke, fret not. A clean, tidy, small apartment is 10 times more chic than a McMansion crowded with expensive, mixed-period furniture and other cacophonous clutter.

Which brings us to the **most important** decorating directive ...

KILL THE CLUTTER

Clutter is the #1 enemy of fabulousness. It offends the eye, distracts the mind, and attracts vermin. Clutter says, "I'm unclean and quite possibly mentally unstable." Tidy up your act and people automatically think you've got it together.

Now, killing clutter is not to be confused with getting organized. Organization is a management objective; clutter-free living is a style mandate. Speaking from personal experience, stylish people are not generally the folks with the alphabetized spice rack. We do, however, have the foresight to keep the dried oregano out of sight.

So, your closets, cabinets, and drawers can be a wreck. Mine are. Just keep all the unnecessary, unsightly objects out of view.

FLATTER YOURSELF WITH COLOR

I'm a big believer in surrounding yourself with colors that flatter you. That goes for your clothes and your crib. I look like death in beige, so there's no way in hell you'll find beige in my wardrobe or my boudoir.

When in doubt, flatter your eyes. Do you have green peepers? Consider decorating with shades of green and/or its opposing color: violet. Blue-eyed babes, go azure and orange. Brown eyes pop with mahogany, purple, and green shades.

Frankly, there are no hard-and-fast rules when it comes to color. Only this fact: Painting is always a good idea. It's the cheapest, fastest way to redo a room. Grab a brush and get busy.

So you're a renter. Signing a lease doesn't mean signing away your right to a fabulous apartment. Every landlord says you can't paint. Screw 'em! Any wall or fixture that was painted when you moved in can be painted to suit your taste. Just make sure that you return it to its original shade of Eggwhite Mousse or whatever the hell it was before you leave.

Quite frankly, I feel the same about hanging stuff on your walls. Hammer away. There's nothing that a little spackle, sandpaper, and white paint won't undo. I once bumped into my New York landlord at the hardware store. I was buying nails and he nearly had a coronary. Whatever. I'm going to patch them up when I leave.

PRETTY UP THE PACKAGING

Dwelling in Western Civilization requires products—products with labels, colors, and shapes that do not reflect your refined sensibility or promote fabulousness. Plopping a bunch of disparately designed products on your countertops is a lot like wearing those free T-shirts companies give away when launching a new motor oil. You wouldn't slap a "Go Mobil 1" logo across your bosom. That same logic applies to products around your house.

THINK:

- Glass or ceramic dispensers for your hand and dish soaps—sanitary and chic
- Wheaties and Cheerios poured from cheery glass containers
- Olive oils and vinegars drizzling from lovely glass bottles
- Sugar bowls, creamers, butter dishes all add a little touch of old-world elegance
- Red wine decanted from a crystal pitcher. No one will know he or she is swilling Château du $5.99. After enough sips, neither will you.

Now, I'm not saying you must confront and recontain every product. Just take control of the items you keep on display every day.

BRING ON THE BLOOMS

Call me a pansy, but I think you should go out of your way to have fresh flowers, at all times, at least in one room of your house. I'm not suggesting you spend $200 a week on elaborate floral arrangements—as fabulous as that would be. Simple clusters of colorful, inexpensive flowers bring life into a room and lighten up your mood. A little bunch of daffodils in the kitchen. A spray of daisies on your desk. An iris stem on your nightstand. Don't you feel better just imagining it?

When I receive a bouquet of fresh flowers, I feel special and loved—unless the arrangement looks like it was purchased in the gift shop of a hospital. Then I feel sorry for the person who gave it to me because they have such bad taste.

Then I feel angry for wasting my time befriending someone with such bad taste. Then I feel guilty for my snobbish thoughts. Then I accept myself for the way I am. It's a four-step process before I even begin rearranging that bouquet, like so:

- Unwrap the offensive bunch and separate the various bits.
- Toss the fern leaves and baby's breath. (Just an FYI: I love ferns outside and inside if potted. I just can't stand 'em in a floral arrangement. Also, I think baby's breath can be awesome when used alone in large sprays.)
- Choose a pretty vessel. A cheap glass vase usually makes your arrangement look cheap. When someone sends you an expensive bouquet, keep the expensive-looking glass vase that usually accompanies it. Teapots, drinking glasses, pitchers, and urns are other aesthetically pleasing options.
- Use a very sharp knife or scissors to snip the stems, keeping in mind the height of your vessel. There's an old "rule" that arrangements should be one and a half times as high as their container. Though you can mostly ignore that rule, do keep proportion in mind. Your flowers shouldn't look like they're too heavy for their vase. On the flip side, you don't want a gigantic vase to overpower a small arrangement.

- Fill the vessel half full with tepid water. Cold water can shock the stems and prevent absorption.
- Arrange the blooms stem by stem into an eye-pleasing, just-gathered-in-the-meadow bunch.
- If you're not a natural at flower arranging—or even if you are—consider buying a few floral frogs (they're like little weights with teeth), some floral foam (that green stuff), and/or some floral tape. A frog or a block of foam thoroughly saturated in water will keep your stems upright, though some people claim they block water from traveling up the flowers' stems. Transparent floral tape, however, arranged in a grid pattern across the top of the vessel will keep flowers upright and drinking freely.
- Change the water as soon as it begins to turn cloudy, or every other day, whichever comes first.

Maybe you live in Anchorage or Grand Forks where fresh flowers are not a staple at the local Piggly Wiggly. Well, force the issue. Bulbs, I mean. The Internet is your floral friend here. Check out gardening sites offering flower bulbs you can easily bring to blossom. Paperwhites, crocuses, and amaryllis are all easy, elegant choices. Even orchids stick around for a month. (My grandmother once said, "Orchids are a good flower for a man." I never asked her why, but her British accent makes everything she says sound like an official memorandum from the Queen herself.)

CURATE YOUR COLLECTIONS

It's time for a national intervention on collecting.

I know you've spent years rustling up every last Marie Osmond doll, Minnie Mouse figurine, or 18th-century monocle. I salute your fortitude. But show some consideration: Don't make me or your guests look at them.

Seriously.

Treasured collections obviously feed your soul. But they are rarely as interesting to others as they are to you. What you think of as evidence of your charming whimsy, your guests might find downright weird. As a general rule, keep your private collecting pleasures private. Very private.

Practice some tough love. Is this a carefully curated collection or is it clutter?

Regardless of how long this affliction, er, I mean collection, has been going on, does it reflect the fabulous person you are today?

If you're a grown woman with 42 stuffed animals on your bed, what does this say to potential suitors? "I'm a wee child of tender heart who loves to cuddle with dusty, smelly, bacteria-laden plush toys. Hold me."

No.

If your collection is more about an investment or family legacy than about passions or décor, then protect it. Wrap your precious cargo in acid-free paper and put it in storage. Keep keepsakes safely away from sunlight, humidity, and my merciless gaze. But if you really love something (and your house is first and foremost about you), display it in an appropriate way where you can enjoy it most—your bedroom or your office, not in the living room.

A NOTE ABOUT BOOKS. As style icon Auntie Mame says, "Books can be so decorative, don't you think?" I do. But books can be dangerous and quickly turn into clutter. Books on the floor are not fabulous. A spray of great books—like this one—on the coffee table is.

DROP GIFT GUILT

Just because your mother gave you a Napoleonic bust, a ceramic bunny, or a Burmese python doesn't mean you have to keep it or display it every time she comes over. First of all, you have to train your friends and family not to give you "decorative objects." They won't listen. But as your fabulousness therapist, I'm giving you permission either to say no or to stow.

When you receive a gift that doesn't fit with your décor, accept it graciously, and then put it in your Goodwill donations box. Get that Italianate candy dish to the needy ASAP. If that tactic would simply kill your dear mother, keep the darn thing but keep it out of sight. If she asks to see it, you'll have it. But you'll also have your aesthetic intact. Not to mention your self-respect. Fabulousness and guilt do not go hand in hand.

GO KEY BOWLING

The key bowl is my one exception to the "no decorative gifts" rule. Everyone—especially gentlemen—needs a small, chic bowl for dropping keys and change. A key bowl is an ideal housewarming gift for a guy. It gives him a goal. Without exception, a full key bowl will contain $18.61 in change—the exact sum necessary for a few frames at the local bowling alley and a pitcher of Bud.

So, man fills bowl. Man goes to coin-counting machine. Man goes bowling. Man is happy.

LIGHTING LEADS TO LOVELINESS

From hosting *What Not to Wear,* I know that a great lighting designer is a best friend forever. If you want to look lovely in your home, you must get your lighting scheme right.

Overhead lighting is the devil. To prevent plunging into the fires of eye-bag hell, install a dimmer on that satanic light switch. If you don't know how, do what I do and get your dad to do it. Somehow dads always know their way around a circuit box. Do whatever you have to do to beat back Beelzebub.

If you have to use dimmed overhead light, remember how Hollywood lights its starlets: a key light on the face, plus fill light gracing the sides of the cheeks from at least two other sources, softening the effect. Floor lamps, table lamps, a sunny window—they're all excellent fillers. Better than Botox.

Mirrors can play a supporting role as well. Placing a mirror where it can catch and bounce light back into a room from a different angle is sheer physics genius.

Candles are a must for entertaining, but why restrict the wicks to parties? Everybody looks better by candlelight. Make lighting candles an everyday occasion. You'll glow with gorgeousness and feel more glamorous.

PASS THE SNIFF TEST

No matter how divine your décor, if your home smells like cat pee, that's all guests will remember. Aroma is a potent design element; overlook aroma at your peril.

Give your house a sniff test when you walk through the door at the end of the day. Musty? Open a window. Feline urine? Toss whatever Fluffy soiled. I don't care if it's an heirloom pillow. A reputation for stench will follow you wherever you go like Pigpen. Not fabulous.

Scented candles add an aesthetic dimension to a space. But don't put one fragrance in the kitchen and different ones in the bedroom and bathroom or your home will smell like a bordello.

Choose classy scented candles (yes, that's code for more pricey brands) that fit with your decorating scheme and suit the season. I'm fond of spicy scents like sage and thyme, or classics that emulate the fragrance of just-washed linen. But candles that are supposed to mimic Grandma's cozy kitchen never quite work. If you want the scent of pumpkin pie wafting through the air, bake one.

GET HORIZONTAL

I'm naturally fabulous at many things, none of which are sports. But if "Arranging Stuff on a Horizontal Surface" ever becomes a nationally sanctioned game, I will be its Tiger Woods.

Mantels, dresser tops, credenzas, shelves—anywhere you find a horizontal surface—are an opportunity for creating sculpture. Think of the area as a seesaw that you have been entrusted to keep level. Balance that baby by paying attention to symmetry vis-à-vis shape, size, and color.

The simplest way to achieve symmetry is to display identical (or nearly identical) objects, evenly spaced, for a soothing visual rhythm. For example: These crystal candlesticks placed in a row across a shelf. I also randomly scattered some fresh fruits, all of which are approximately the same size, for some added color and visual interest. Should you try this at home, remove the fruit before it rots, lest you awaken one night to the sounds of a sewer rat chomping on an Anjou pear.

You can also use items in similar shades of the same color to create an arresting tableau. Here I arranged blue glass and porcelain vases along the shelf, varying the sizes, shapes and textures just a bit. The common color, evenly spread along the plane, balances the arrangement. Obviously, this would work with any color palette—except flesh tones, particularly that of Hummels. Die, you freaky homunculi, die!

When showing off an unrelated grouping of stuff, consider each piece's visual "weight." For example, these two black gourds look heavy, even though they're actually quite light, while the white orchids opposite them appear to be light and airy, despite the fact that the pot they're in weighs about 20 pounds. So, the taller orchid is balanced by the smaller gourds. Similarly, the pink daisy, with its bright color and texture has the same visual impact as the three smaller red goblets. Take a step back, and see if the seesaw teeters. Nope? You're golden.

HANG UP PICTURE HANG-UPS

Are your pictures in a permanent state of paralysis? Propped up against walls? Hidden in closets? You are too fabulous to have hang-ups about hanging up your pictures. Let's begin.

FIRST, decide what your consistent statement will be: frames or pictures.

If you're mixing up different styles of frames, choose pictures with a consistent visual thread. Same photographer. Or all black and white. Or all color. Or, choose the same style of frame and mix up the content.

SECOND, pick your spot.

For a jaw-droppingly chic conversation starter, take one area and make it floor-to-ceiling, wall-to-wall pictures. Not up to creating a bonanza of imagery? Fine. A careful arrangement of pictures will do quite nicely.

SO, NEXT, prepare your jigsaw-puzzle pieces.

What? You thought I was going to send you waving that hammer willy-nilly? No, this is a precision operation, my friend. Do not rush it. This will be the only moment when the phrase "get crafty" applies.

First, trace the shape of your frames onto kraft paper. Cut the various shapes out. Then tape them onto your wall—using low-stick tape—in your proposed arrangement. Step way back and have a look. Do the corners line up? Does the design scream clever symmetry?

You may proceed.

What's great about having the paper pictures up is, you can nail through the paper with confidence. No juggling that heavy Mapplethorpe nude in one hand, sharp objects in the other. Once you've got it nailed, simply tear the paper away, replace it with your masterpiece, and repeat.

Don't restrict your hangings to paintings and photos. Add mirrors or textiles to the mix. What goes up can come down, so take a risk already.

FURNISH WITH PROPORTION

Just as you pay attention to proportion in clothing (big prints overwhelm small frames; small jewelry looks dinky on larger frames), pick your furnishings with that same eye.

If you're decorating a small space, don't shove a huge, boldly printed couch in there along with a patterned rug and plaid wall hanging. Sensory overload is not fabulous. You want to make one strong statement and then support it by toning down the rest of the room's "outfit."

So, if you want to put bold, fanciful wallpaper in a smaller space, go for it. But make everything else—sofa, rug, lamps—understated, keeping the proportion. If you're lucky enough to have humongous rooms to play in, play big. A tiny lighting fixture and small chairs will simply get lost in the space. Think larger proportions and bolder colors. Remember my six-foot black antler chandelier? It would be a disaster in my Manhattan apartment, but at Le Lodge, it's perfect.

Now, as a veteran flea marketeer and Dumpster diver, I'm all for cheap furnishings. But before you pick up that adorable end table and throw it in the trunk, ask the clutter question: Is this worth the space? Money's not the issue here; it's about preventing public enemy #1 from crossing your threshold.

And second: Can I make this work with my design scheme? Mismatched items can absolutely work together, but a fabulous room needs some cohesion. If your coffee table, chairs, end tables, sofa, and dining table are from different eras and made of different types of wood, consider painting them all the same color for a more unified look.

REARRANGE REGULARLY

As a kid, I used to rearrange my bedroom furniture every couple of weeks. Granted, I was a very special child, but I am a big believer in regularly changing up the scenery.

Just as you reevaluate your wardrobe each season, take a look at your furniture and mix it up at least twice a year. Say, every spring and fall when Daylight Saving Time hits. It's perfect. A whole weekend to check your smoke detectors, move your furniture, sweep out the dust bunnies, and reset your clocks.

You might find that conversation flows anew, once you've made the seating all about looking at each other instead of Mary Hart. Which brings me to . . .

CONTROL ELECTRONIC DISTRACTIONS

I'm not about to disrespect TV; TV made us friends, you and me. However, I don't think the television should be the master of any room, nor should it dictate the rhythms of your home. Use your living room to live in, your kitchen to eat in, your bedroom to cuddle-'n'-sleep in, and, if possible, create a media room for watching TV.

If the box must live in the living room, hide it when it's not in use. Put the TV in an armoire along with the stereo, DVD player, and the rest of your electronic gadgets. Or, toss a colorful blanket over the whole mess and call it serape sculpture.

In this digital age, we are surrounded by unsightly cords and cables for the TV, Internet, phone chargers ad infinitum. It's a visual plague. Bribe the cable guy to at least use neutral-toned cables you can paint over.

For electronics, stash cords behind furniture. Try using those little cord caddy things sold at the hardware store that can help you prevent a jumbled octopus back there. And pray for a truly wireless future.

PUT KIDS IN THEIR PLACE

Kids are precious angels from heaven, but they should not lord over your décor. Your kids' stuff and your kids' taste belong in your kids' bedrooms.

Call me a heretic, but I believe refrigerators are for keeping Sauvignon Blanc chilled to 38 degrees, not for displaying children's art. Put a corkboard up in Johnny's room and pin his works up where he can enjoy them. Same thing goes for trophies, awards, and other evidence of your offspring's excellence.

And toys. How many parents have their fabulousness quotient disastrously diminished due to their entire dwelling being under Barbie siege? If you have space for a dedicated playroom, use it. Throw those kids and toys into the basement or backyard. They'll be fine. Look how I turned out.

NURTURE NEGLECTED SPACES

You're paying big bucks for your house or apartment, but are you effectively using every square inch of it?

THINK:

Front door and foyer. A snappy welcome mat starts your color statement. Once inside, the first space you see upon entering your abode and the last space you see before setting off should have some personality. This is a great place to hang treasured photos or add a splash of pattern.

A narrow hallway. This is an ideal spot to take a risk with color.

Flip-side of a cabinet or closet door. Rather than foul the eye with coupons and bulletins out in the open, mount corkboards on the inside of cupboards you open every day, like where you keep the coffee cups.

Take a look up high and down low in a room. Is there an opportunity to play with that space? I'm not talking about wallpaper borders. Perish the thought. But how about some colorful bookshelves? A row of ceramic pots? A fuchsia fisherman's net?

TREAT WINDOWS WITH RESPECT

Just as not every ensemble requires jewelry, not every window needs drapery. If a window offers a gorgeous, private view, skip the curtains or blinds. Dance naked before the forest, you nymph.

If you're staring at brick walls or Mr. Peabody's prying eyes, give your window a chic cover-up. But beware fussy window treatments. Ruffles do nothing but ruffle my feathers. Avoid.

Shaggy, ugly blinds should hit the bin. Replace them or try a rotating cast of curtains instead.

Hang a new set while the others are being dry-cleaned. The Internet has sources for every conceivable window treatment. Pick a site with a money-back guarantee, and go to town.

Short on cash? New, colorful sheets can be hemmed and put through any rod. Not a seamstress? Have your dry cleaner do it for a few bucks.

The scale of your curtains can create some intriguing illusions in a room. For example, if you have a smallish window on a big wall, creating a curtain to go all the way across the space horizontally can trick the eye into thinking there's a huge span of glass behind the fabric. So clever.

FLOORS THAT FLOOR

Wall-to-wall carpet is generally not fabulous. Even a crappy wood floor is better than stinky, parasite-ridden pile carpet. And, pet owners, there should be a law forbidding Fido from coming anywhere near such beastly floor coverings.

If you can rip out the carpet, do it. Whatever you find under there has got to be an improvement. Woods can be sanded or stained or just mopped; cement can be treated and painted.

If you're in a rental, get a steam cleaner and scrub the bejesus out of it. Hopefully, the carpet is at least a neutral tone so you can throw a colorful rug over it. (Baby blue shag? Pass the smelling salts.)

Overall, you should proceed with caution when it comes to rugs. The right rug (often the most expensive rug you could ever freakin' imagine) can unite a room like nothing else. The wrong rug, however, can make a room look smaller, or will draw the eye down to the floor, where it will no doubt spot the daily debris of crumbs, hair, and dust. You don't need the aggravation.

So, as always, when in doubt, leave it out.

ROOM-BY-ROOM EXTRAS

By now your wardrobe features a fabulous mix of color, texture, pattern, and shine. So should each room in your home. Here are some easy ways to spruce up specific spaces . . .

BEDROOM

The chic do not dress their beds from Bed-in-a-Bag linen sets. Consult your color palette, and pick your bedding from different sources, staying within the hues. Mix up designers, patterns, and textures for a fresh look that showcases your creativity in the bedroom.

Let's say you love a cheery floral duvet. Add solid pillowcases and perhaps a lighty striped sheet that uses a color or two from your bedspread's bouquet. I call it the Tony Orlando & Dawn Technique. Pick one strong, lead pattern and add two back-up singers. The fabulous always make their beds the moment they get up. Do we like to? No. But remember, your rooms create a vibe that affects your whole being. Especially your boudoir.

If you come home after a hard day and see a sloppy, unmade bed, do you feel fabulous? Thought not. How much sexier would you feel stepping into your day knowing you could invite Mr. Right Now right on over should your fabulous paths cross at that after-work cocktail party? Getting that bed made increases your chances of getting laid. How much more incentive do you need?

Be prepared.

To ensure a fabulous first impression:

Eliminate overhead lighting. Candles, a small lamp, or your incandescent glow will more than suffice.

Clear your nightstand of everything except a photo of dear friends or family, the one book you're reading, an alarm clock, and flowers. Condoms, lip balm, and mints should be tucked in a nearby drawer, not put on display.

Put your clothes in the closet or laundry bag the minute you take them off. Delays are allowed only if someone else is removing your clothing.

BATHROOM

In a word, bleach.

You already know how I feel about the various duties performed in the WC. The most effective way to brighten up the room meant for dirty business is to be ridiculously anal about cleanliness. Sparkling is the standard; accept no compromise.

Take every product off of the sink and countertop except hand soap (which you've already put in a pretty pump, right?). Stow everything in the medicine cabinet and drawers. Makeup, cologne, toothbrushes, tampons—I'm glad you have these things; I just don't want to see them.

Fresh white towels make any bathroom look like an upscale spa. Buy 'em by the dozen and donate them to Goodwill at the first sign of dinginess. Sounds extravagant, but it's not really that expensive. And towels always seem to be on sale.

Grungy, moldy grout sends me into a tailspin. Either replace the grout surrounding your tiles (hardware stores have kits) or scrub it like Lady Macbeth. Just make the cruddy go away.

Put up a new shower curtain every few months. (Need I remind you to launder or replace the liner every month? Mildew is a kissing cousin to bubonic plague; stop the epidemic in its tracks, for goodness sakes.) Think of your shower curtain as a space for a bold color statement. You can find thousands of patterns and styles on Web sites, and since most curtains are about $30 or less, there's no excuse for boring.

And please hang up that shower curtain with metal hooks. Plastic rings look tacky and cultivate mold spores.

KITCHEN

Don't let devices cut away at your counter space. Counters should be reserved for the VIMs (very important machines) you use every day. Coffeemakers and microwaves probably make the cut. But keep the blender, salad spinner, toaster, food processor, and the like out of sight.

Same thing goes for pots, pans, and mixing bowls. No guest needs to admire your copper-bottom double boiler hanging on some hook. Let Henry admire your panache at dipping strawberries in dark chocolate from the double boiler, when the time comes.

Pressing the put-away point further, food belongs in the fridge or in the cupboard.

If you hate something, paint it white. Counters, cabinets, floors. Sanity in a can, that's what white paint is. Believe me.

Congratulations!

You now know how to decorate fabulously and are officially FREAKIN' FABULOUS!

Seat 29A

From ~~The Desk of~~

Clinton Kelly

(Business Class was sold out.)

Dear Reader,

We've come to the end of our time together and I feel as though I should share with you some parting thoughts.

I'm sure you imagine me writing them while sipping a latte and eating a baguette on a balcony overlooking the Mediterranean. Close. I'm somewhere above what I think may be greater Baltimore—who can tell—on a flight from New York to Fort Lauderdale. You see, I'm doing a personal appearance in Boca Raton in a few hours. Then, I'm hopping on a puddle-jumper this evening to Orlando for another meet-and-greet at a mall there tomorrow. A guy's gotta eat.

The nearby lavatory is emitting a most unholy stench, the man in front of me has reclined his seat so much that I think we may have technically reached third base, and I just realized that I left my cell-phone charger on my nightstand at home. Yeah, that's just great.

Where am I going with all this? Oh, I don't know. Let me take a few minutes to think about it.

[Insert 10-minute pause.]

OK, I'm back and I've realized my point:

Fabulousity is not just a way of life; it's a state of being. It's not just about saying all the right things, wearing all the right things, and doing all the right things. It transcends all that. You are only fabulous if your head is fully invested in it!

So what if the toilet is overflowing! That doesn't make me less fabulous.

So what if you're the guy who has to clean it when we land! That doesn't make you less fabulous.

You can be fabulous no matter what your circumstances. Just pay attention to how you are living your freakin' life! Helping your elderly neighbor shovel her snowy driveway makes you more fabulous. Spitting your chewing gum out on the sidewalk makes you less fabulous. Eating a double cheeseburger with fries and a shake every once in a while is fabulous. Eating fast food five times a week is not. Studying Mandarin just for the heck of it: fabulous. Watching eight hours of TV a day: not so much. Picking up an antique chair at a flea market: fabulous. Bragging about the value of your Ming vase collection: not.

Are you getting this?

More than anything, you are fabulous if you treat people with respect and encourage them to develop their own fabulous qualities. So, try not to be a jerk. And send your grandmother flowers every once in a while for no particular reason. Just tell the florist to hold the baby's breath.

That's all. Have a nice life. Seriously.

Christian

I love America.
Well, most of it.

Acknowledgments

Anyone who thinks he can be fabulous on his own is just plain full of it. I'd like to thank the following people for their help in making this book come to fruition.

TRICIA BOCZKOWSKI and JENNIFER BERGSTROM
of Simon Spotlight Entertainment, some seriously fierce publishing broads who conveniently like the sauce as much as I do.

MEGAN LESSER,
a creative genius with a charming tendency to misplace invoices.

GABRIELLE REVERE,
a spunky photographer with a penchant for young, slim, hairless men.

JENNIFER ROBINSON,
an energetic publicist who would run me into the ground if I let her.

JANE ARCHER,
a supremely talented graphic designer with a ferociously curly mane.

ROBERT CLYDE ANDERSON,
a chic illustrator with lots of patience.

DEANNA NICKEL, KURT LOWRY, and MERILYN MITCHELL,
the ultimate glam squad.

LAUREN KELLER GALIT,
a totally chill agent who's not even a jerk.

JACKIE ECKHOUSE,
a lawyer with an actual soul.

CHRISTA BOURG,
a thorough researcher who's
hit-or-miss when it comes to her shoes.

You will be mine
Stealing an orchid from work

CREDITS

All photographs by Gabrielle Revere unless otherwise noted.
All illustrations by Robert Clyde Anderson unless otherwise noted.

STYLE CREDITS
Creative Director
Megan Lesser

Food Stylist
Suzette Kiminski

Styling Assistants
Allison Berlin
Cate Sheehy
Zoe Sundra

Hair
Kurt Lowry
Merylin Mitchell

Makeup
Deanna Nickel

FRONT COVER
Tuxedo by Zegna
Christian Louboutin heels from the Jess Neff Collection
Thank-you note from Cranes

BACK COVER
Shoes provided by Jeffrey New York
Jewelry from Henri Bendel

INTRODUCTION
p. x Pattern by Jane Archer

DRESS
p. 29 Bra image CSA Printstock Illustration/Veer
p. 31 Wedding dress by Judd Wadell
p. 44 Jessica Tandy: Miss Daisy studio/Photofest
p. 44 Humphrey Bogart: Photofest
p. 45 Mother Teresa: Photofest
p. 45 Mao Tse-Tung: Photofest
p. 45 Matthew McConaughey: Photofest
pp. 46-47 Fabulous shoes provided by Jeffrey New York

Special thanks to
Bulga Bags
Jeffrey NY
Jennifer Miller jewelry
Supplements NYC
Zappos.com

Models
Cara
David
Margo
Ellen
Clinton
Fern
Jennifer
Sarah

SPEAK
p. 58 Phone image, courtesy of the Scott Russo Archive
p. 68 Telephone © Photodisc
p. 74 Polaroid taken by Megan Lesser
p. 74 Winking lady image, © Wonderstock

BEHAVE
Hand model: Serena
Baked goods from Sarabeth's, Chelsea Market
Candy from Economy Candy

p. 78 Fork and knife image, courtesy of the Scott Russo Archive
p. 79 Background wallpaper from Studio Print Works
p. 82 Jewelry provided by Lia Sophia
p. 83 Vintage salt and pepper shakers from Mr. Pinks, New York City
p. 99 "Poof" illustrations by Megan Lesser
p. 102 Crying women image, CSA Mod Art/Veer
p. 106 Yves Delorme tablecloth, silverware provided by Mrs. Sybil Pollet
p. 108 Gumball machine, plan59.com
p. 111 Flipping couple, © Wonderstock

Jewelry provided by
Alexis Bittar
Jennifer Miller
Lia Sophia
Supplements

Restaurant Interiors shot at
The Harrison Restaurant
355 Harrison Street
New York City

Models
Eileen
Jess
Kevin
Shana
Brian
Melissa
Serena
Megan's Legs

ETIQUETTE
American/Continental
Serena's hands
J.L. Coquet plate from Barneys
Placemat by Bernadaut provided by
Mrs. Sybil Pollet
Flatware by Crate & Barrel
Candy by Economy Candy
Ring by Lia Sophia
Bracelet by Alexis Bittar

pp. 92-93
Model: Merylin
Oyster
Top by Chaiken
Earrings by Lia Sophia
Ring (stylist's own)

Model: Sarah
Lamb
Top by Banana Republic
Lamb by Chelsea diner

Model: Shana
Asparagus
Cream dress by Chloé & Reese
Jewelry provided by Lia Sophia
Asparagus by Park Restaurant

Clinton eating spaghetti
Bowl by Missoni at Barneys Chelsea Passage
Pattern: Margherita by Missoni
Flatware by Carl Mertens
Shirt by Etro
Sweater-vest by Paul Smith
Spaghetti by Chelsea Diner

p. 106 Cellphone/Lateness
Clinton's hand
Yves Delorme tablecloth and napkin (C&B)
ABC Carpet & Home
Bakelite flatware (stylist's own), France

p. 109 Serena with ambrosia in tupperware
Candy by Economy Candy
Top by Lily Pulitzer
Skirt by Nanette Lapore
Earrings by Miguel Ases (stylist's own)
Charm bracelets (stylist's own)

EAT
Food styling by Suzette Kaminski

p. 114 Pot, courtesy of the Scott Russo Archive
p. 114 Pattern by Jane Archer
p. 117 Alarm Clock © Photodisc
Photo of Vintage starburst clock, courtesy of the Scott Russo Archive
Clock Illustrations by Jane Archer
p. 118 Piñata © Photodisc
p. 124 Knife set image, courtesy of the Scott Russo Archive
p. 124 American Meat Institute advertisement, 1947, plan49.com
p. 127 Skillet image, courtesy of the Scott Russo Archive
p. 128 Toaster image, courtesy of the Scott Russo Archive
p. 130 Women grilling image, courtesy of the Scott Russo Archive
p. 130/131 Meat pattern, CSA Printstock Illustration/Veer
p. 131 Vintage plate image, courtesy of the Scott Russo Archive
p. 131 Stack sandwich illustration, © Wonderstock
p. 134 Pot, courtesy of the Scott Russo Archive
p. 136 Meat advertisement, plan49.com
p. 137 Question mark man, © Wonderstock
p. 137 Polaroid taken by Megan Lesser

Olives
J.L. Coquet plate
Textured placemat at Barneys Chelsea Passage
Olives from Chelsea Market

p. 117 Hollandaise sauce
Plate by Sydney Albertini
Flatware by Match

p. 120 French omelet
Plate by Fornasetti
Flatware (stylist's own)

p. 122 Vinaigrette
Vintage Gucci gravy boat (stylist's own)

p. 129 Poached Egg
Clinton's number candle holders
Yves Delorme tablecloth
Eduardo Garza silver tray

DRINK
p. 150 Concrete texture © Photodisc
p. 152 Carafe, courtesy of the Scott Russo Archive

ENTERTAIN
Chapter opener: Megan's Legs
p. 165 Lobster bowl image, courtesy of the Scott Russo Archive
p. 167 Jumping couple illustration, © Wonderstock
p. 169 Pattern by Jane Archer
p. 175 Welcome mat © Photodisc
p. 177 Marbles © Photodisc

DECORATE
Chapter opener
Blue vases by The End of History, Hudson Street, NYC
Ceramic floral vase, Clinton's own

p. 216 Dollhouse image, courtesy of the Scott Russo Archive
p. 216 Pattern by Jane Archer
p. 217 Clinton's chandelier photograph, © Michael Kodas/The Hartfort Courant
p. 218 Frame man illustration, © Wonderstock
p. 221 Wallpaper from Studio Print Works
p. 227 Goards from http://gottagettagourd.blogspot.com/
p. 228 Frame © Photodisc
p. 230 TV man, © Wonderstock
p. 231 Kids in pool image, courtesy of the Scott Russo Archive
p. 231 Kids cop car image, courtesy of the Scott Russo Archive
p. 233 Upright vacuum image, courtesy of the Scott Russo Archive
p. 236 Tiles © Photodisc
p. 237 Mixer image, courtesy of the Scott Russo Archive
Anthropologie white pitcher
Studio works wall paper
p. 238 Airplane window image from Getty Images
p. 243 Drawing of "Spider-Man" by Hector A. Cabrera, (age 7).

Mantle
Goards, http://gottagettagourd.blogspot.com/
Blue vases by The End of History, Hudson Street, NYC

All one color/ Blue vases/ Monocramatic/ Grouping
The End of History, Hudson Street, NYC

Fruit and Candlesticks
Holiday/Elegant
Anthropologie candlesticks

Bedding
Coral cotton blanket from West Elm
Velvet/Linen pillow from West Elm
Calvin Klein floral sheet/duvet cover from Macy's

Cream/Beige Yves Delorme damask
Leather pillow (stylist's own)
D'Isle ruscched pillow, ABC Carpet & Home
Pillow from West Elm

Geometric print sheet from Area
Calvin Klein printed sheet from Macy's
Blue pillow from Target

Yves Delorme blue-and-yellow pillow
Cashmere blanket from ABC Carpet & Home
Calvin Klein bedding from Macy's